Praise for *Eat Happy*

"No one makes food as happy and healthy as Anna! Her cookbooks are amongst my family's favorites."

—Dr. Mindy Pelz, international bestselling author of *Fast Like a Girl* and founder of The Reset Academy

"If you're ever lucky enough to have my Mama or Anna Vocino cook you a meal in person like I have, you will realize that you are one of the luckiest people on the planet. With *Eat Happy Italian*, you now have the best of both worlds. But wait, it gets better . . . these recipes are also NSNG® approved by me to be great Italian low-carb options to enjoy."

—Vinnie Tortorich, cohost of the *Fitness Confidential* podcast and founder of NSNG®

"As the cost of dining out rockets to the moon, honing your cooking skills and learning how to make simple, delicious meals at home is a very smart move. The ever-talented Anna Vocino creates some of the tastiest real food recipes around. When you crave a hearty, healthy, nutrient-dense meal with Italian flair, you can't do better than *Eat Happy Italian*."

—Abel James, *New York Times* bestselling author of *The Wild Diet*, podcast host, and musician

"My go-to choice for gifts are always books written by friends, and I can't wait to gift Anna Vocino's *Eat Happy Italian*. As a doctor, a big part of my day is negotiating healthy lifestyle habits to deaf ears. Gluten-free and low-carb eating plans are healthy, but rarely tasty. Ms. Vocino has figured it out, and in Italian. I prescribe the frico and mortadella dip with the parmesan chips. If we're friends, no need to buy her book. Everyone else, invest in a most tasty cookbook experience. Doctor's orders!"

—Dr. David Kipper, host of the *Bedside Matters* podcast and coauthor of *Override*

"Delicious, classic, healthy, Italian. These are the first four words that come to mind when I think about *Eat Happy Italian*. As someone who loves Italian food, but is also gluten-free and low-carb, this book allows me to still enjoy some of my favorite dishes without compromising my diet or my indulgences. I highly recommend this for anyone looking for healthy Italian recipes that taste amazing."

—Quentin Vennie, cofounder of Equitea, author, and wellness expert

"I love Italian food and making it delicious and nutritious while being low-carb is always a challenge. But, no more! Anna Vocino has created the perfect cookbook! This is one I can feel good recommending to my patients who have been following Keto-Green and know they will have great results. Get and share this book with friends!"

—Dr. Anna Cabeca, OBGYN, *USA Today* bestselling author of *The Hormone Fix*

"Anna Vocino is a magical unicorn who has brought fun back into the kitchen. My gluten-free six year old loves these Italian recipes and doesn't even miss the bread or pasta!"

—Andrea Anders, actor (HBO's *Bookies* and Netflix's *That 90's Show*)

"Anna has been cooking for me since I was 22 years old, so when she came out with her own line of cookbooks, it wasn't a surprise. In *Eat Happy Italian*, she has gone back to her Italian roots and created a beautiful book . . . I like to leaf through it and fantasize about what I'll make next. Luckily, the book is pretty resistant to drool stains. I'm one of the lucky ones to experience this incredible woman's nurturing and friendship IRL, but when you cook Anna's food, you'll feel that love, too."

—Sarah Baker, actor (Netflix's *The Kominsky Method*)

"Anna Vocino has solved one of the toughest challenges that I experience as a physician focusing on metabolic health and diabetes management . . . making healthy Italian food! Many of my patients happen to be Italian and they often say, 'Doc, I want to eat great-tasting food even if I die a few years sooner. It is worth it.' Now they can have both. I have shared Anna's products and recipes with my friends, family, and patients. Now they can have the highest quality real food that they can prepare and enjoy with their families. Nothing beats an authentic Italian meal made with fresh and healthy ingredients. We won't ruin their pleasure by letting them know how healthy it is, we'll just allow them to eat happy and live longer lives! I recommend this book to everyone that I know and am sure that we will have more friends visiting for outstanding Italian food (and hopefully great conversation). This book should be a staple in every household. *Mangia bene!*"

—Brian Lenzkes, MD, cohost of the *LowCarbMD Podcast*

EAT HAPPY
ITALIAN

Also by Anna Vocino

*Eat Happy: Gluten-Free, Grain-Free, Low-Carb Recipes
for a Joyful Life*

*Eat Happy Too: 160+ New Gluten-Free, Grain-Free,
Low-Carb Recipes for a Joyful Life*

EAT HAPPY ITALIAN

101 Gluten-Free, Grain-Free, Low-Carb Recipes
for Living La Bella Vita

Anna Vocino

BenBella

BenBella Books, Inc.
Dallas, TX

Eat Happy Italian copyright © 2024 by Anna Vocino
Photographs by Anna Vocino

NSNG is a registered trademark owned by Vinnie Tortorich.

BenBella Books, Inc.
10440 N. Central Expressway
Suite 800
Dallas, TX 75231
benbellabooks.com
Send feedback to feedback@benbellabooks.com

BenBella is a federally registered trademark.

Printed in China
10 9 8 7 6 5 4 3 2 1

Library of Congress Control Number: 2023059703
ISBN 9781637745298 (trade paperback)
ISBN 9781637745304 (electronic)

Editing by Claire Schulz and Ruth Strother
Copyediting by Karen Wise
Proofreading by Ashley Casteel and Cape Cod Compositors, Inc.
Indexing by Debra Bowman
Text design and composition by Endpaper Studio
Cover design by Morgan Carr
Cover photography by Anna Vocino
Printed by Dream Colour

For Rose, Elvira, Angela, Margaret, Lea, Diane, Caroline, Leslie, and Lucy.

Metti il tuo cuore nelle mie mani e sarai felice.

Put your heart in my hands, and you'll be happy.

CONTENTS

PREFACE

Hi there. I'm Anna Vocino, a cookbook author and purveyor of fine foods. I have a supercool day job as a voice talent in commercials, film, TV, and video games. This day job funds my passion projects of podcasting, writing books, and, recently, launching a sauce and spice company. I believe strongly in the power of good food. I want to feed the world delicious dinners, mostly Italian, that can nourish our bodies by way of cutting out processed sugars and grains.

I started my career working on camera and constantly being on a diet. It was crazy-making. The yo-yo of it all was untenable, and when I started producing and cohosting the *Fitness Confidential* podcast in 2012 with Vinnie Tortorich, I had no idea how much knowing him would change my life.

Vinnie is the creator of NSNG®, which stands for No Sugars No Grains. It's a commonsense, real food approach to eating that cuts out processed sugars and grains. If you want to modify the way you eat beyond NSNG, then have at it, but the foundation is cutting out sugars and grains.

Having been diagnosed with celiac disease in 2002, I was already eating gluten free and blogging delicious recipes in my spare time as a distraction from the unpredictability that comes with working in the entertainment industry. Slowly but surely, I was putting on weight and had no idea why. I kept thinking that if I would just diet more and count calories harder, I'd lose the weight. Turns out eating gluten free does not equate to weight loss when you're overconsuming processed sugars and grains (which I was). I didn't realize I was playing a game of hormonal roulette—a game I would never win.

When I started podcasting with Vinnie, I reluctantly gave his NSNG plan a shot. Side note: It's not even really a plan. You just cut out processed sugars and grains. That's it. No counting, no dieting, no weighing portions. After years and years of unsuccessful on-and-off dieting, I was willing to try anything. I went hardcore with NSNG and never looked back.

I changed the entire focus of my blog and recipes to be low carb. Turns out, other people wanted to do NSNG, but they needed to figure out what to eat. I could help with that. I published the first *Eat Happy* cookbook in 2016 and the second, *Eat Happy Too*, in 2019. I named the books *Eat Happy* because I had changed my brain chemistry for the better when I got rid of processed sugars and grains.

I had watched my mom struggle with her sugar addiction and depression over the years, and eventually she succumbed to a systemic infection that her organs weren't strong enough to fight due to the damage done over the years by sugar and diet sodas. I was lucky enough to be by her side in 2014 when she passed from this world, and I vowed to do my part to help others learn about the dangers of processed food. Someday I'll go into more detail about the impact this had on me (as it does for everyone who's lost a parent).

One day in 2019, a podcast fan reached out to me and told me that he had lost a lot of weight cooking out of my books and that he was a food manufacturer who wanted to produce my tomato sauce. I agreed, and we went back and forth developing the original recipe. I had to make sure it tasted exactly like my recipe, as if I walked into your kitchen and made it for you. In August 2020, I launched the Eat Happy Kitchen Tomato Basil Marinara to my podcast audience, and it sold like wildfire. That man, Mike Weeks, has been instrumental in helping me create all five sauce flavors that we now sell. We started with the original Tomato Basil Marinara, a recipe you'll find in this book. Then we launched Pink Crema (a vodka sauce with no vodka), Puttanesca Sauce, Arrabbiata Spicy Marinara, and the seasonal favorite Pumpkin Marinara. Now Eat Happy Kitchen is launching into grocery chains across

the US, manufacturing the sauces in larger kettles, and growing expo-
nentially. I'm forever grateful to Mike for reaching out to me in 2019 to
help me kick off what has become larger than I ever anticipated.

All my blogging, podcasting, and publishing come from my desire
to be a resource for people, and I want all my recipes and the food that
I sell to be made with the highest-quality, best-tasting ingredients
out there.

INTRODUCTION

This book is my collection of Italian and Italian American food favorites. There are of course a bajillion more recipes that couldn't fit into this book, plus many more that I didn't want to tinker with if the low-carb version wouldn't do the recipe justice. So I created and curated my favorites to share with you in hopes that you will make them for your friends and family, thus keeping this circle of food love expanding outward into the world.

My grandparents and millions of Italian immigrants came to America and shared their culinary culture. Many of their recipes became classics and evolved into some of our favorite Italian American dishes, such as meatballs and chicken parmesan. I love making low-carb versions of not only Italian American dishes but also my favorite Italian dishes that I have enjoyed time and time again on my travels throughout Italy. Most of my favorite Italian dishes were made in the homes of friends and the nonnas of friends, who love to cook for anyone who walks through their door.

Since Italian food is an important part of my heritage, plus I own a pasta sauce company, I have already published some kick-butt low-carb Italian food recipes. You'll find updated versions of some of those in these pages. The entire focus of this book is Italian and Italian American recipes, so I got to go deep with my favorite classics as well as develop new recipes that I hope you'll enjoy.

Adapting for a Low-Carb Diet and Shopping for Ingredients

I have a tremendous amount of video content on YouTube (@AnnaVocino), Instagram (@annavocino), and Substack (annavocino.substack.com) demonstrating low-carb cooking techniques, explaining the details behind what works and what doesn't, and discussing at length how to stock your pantry, grocery shop, and read ingredient lists and labels. If you are new to low carb, I want to make sure you have the tools you need to succeed.

When grocery shopping, buy the highest-quality meat, produce, and dairy that's available and affordable. I'm not gonna lie, meat is definitely more expensive than grains, but I think reallocating my dollars to a healthy, delicious diet is way less expensive in the long run than doctors' bills or medications. I try not to call for anything unfamiliar or difficult to source in the US in my recipes. I want this food to be accessible to everyone.

Always remember to look at labels before buying anything, even that mayo you've bought for years. Companies change formulas all the time, so you want to make sure your store-bought goodies from the center aisle—think sauces, canned and jarred ingredients, and the like—haven't had any sugars or grains added. In my recipes, I specify no-sugar-added for ingredients where many brands sneak sugar into their products, such as canned diced tomatoes and coconut milk.

I am not a scientist, doctor, or researcher. If you are interested in the science behind low carb, please read the numerous books written by people who are experts in the field (I have a list on my website, annavocino.com). I am here to offer you recipes and meal ideas once you have shifted your paradigm to a real-food way of eating (and trust me, it's pretty delicious). Here are a few notes on some items that you'll want stocked in your kitchen.

Olive Oil

Use real extra-virgin olive oil. You might need to do some research here because according to a UC Davis olive oil study from 2010, about 69 percent of olive oils tested failed to meet accepted extra-virgin olive oil standards.

CARCIOFI ALLA GRIGLIA
€28,90

€ 18,90

€ 17,90

I use Villa Cappelli extra-virgin olive oil—try it for the best olive oil you'll ever taste. Then thank me later on Instagram. You'll find more on my love of Villa Cappelli in the dessert chapter (of all places), in the recipe for Olive Oil Cake with Limoncello Glaze (page 195).

I avoid using the following extremely processed seed oils: canola, sunflower, safflower, cottonseed, corn, or soybean oil. They are great for industrial applications but should be avoided whenever possible in your food.

Sauces

I've been making my own marinara for almost thirty years (wow, I'm old). I published my marinara recipe in my first cookbook, in my second cookbook, on my website, and in this cookbook as well.

Italian food by its nature has a lot of tomato-based sauces incorporated into recipes. Wherever possible, I let you know when you can use a jar of store-bought sauce. While I know for a fact my company makes the highest-quality, best-tasting jarred sauce, you never have to buy it to make these recipes. You'll find the full recipes for those red sauces in the Make Your Own chapter. I publish these recipes because I want everyone to have access to these delicious flavors. But if you happen to be in your local grocery store and see a jar of Eat Happy Kitchen Tomato Basil Marinara on the shelves, I hope you'll pick it up and enjoy it just as much as if it were homemade (yes, it tastes that good).

Salt

I love Redmond Real Salt and Maldon salt, but any sea salt will do. Check the labels to be sure nothing else has been added. If you are afraid of salt, don't be. Salt is our friend, and salt gives us flavor. In most of my recipes, unless there's a specific measurement of salt, I will have "salt and pepper" in the ingredient list and then will tell you the various points during the instructions to season your creation with salt and freshly ground black pepper. ABT—always be tasting—to make sure you have enough salt and flavor.

Wine

A lot of Italian cuisine uses a splash or so of leftover or inexpensive wine to help deepen the flavor of certain dishes. I've found a way to use a combination of white or red wine vinegar and chicken broth to achieve the same goal. The reason for this is that when some folks go low carb, they don't keep wine on hand as much, and I don't want to make anyone buy a bottle just to use half a cup in a recipe. I came up with this substitute because it works perfectly, and it uses common ingredients you will see throughout my books. If you do choose to use wine, that is totally fine! The alcohol cooks off, and it's safe to serve to kids. I live in wine country now, so I have no shortage of wine, but I also prefer to save my wine for a splurge.

Breakfast

Old-school Italian cookbooks don't have a breakfast chapter but instead include egg recipes as a section in the main course chapter. Italians love to serve eggs for a simple lunch or dinner and, to be honest, they don't eat much breakfast. We Americans love us some breakfast and brunch, so I included all my egg recipes in the Breakfast chapter, plus some fun twists on classics—and even a low-carb pancake.

Sweeteners

If you are looking for a diet book, you will not find that here. I make real food. I don't count macros or calories. And when I make a dessert, I make it with the least amount of real sugar possible to make it what it's intended to be—a sweet treat. I have sweet treats only rarely, but when I do, I enjoy them, then I get right back on plan.

Only you know yourself. If you know that by making one of the sweets recipes you will go on a six-month carb bender, then please do yourself a favor and don't make it! I believe strongly in a well-balanced life, but only you know the difference between your own enjoyment of food and your own triggers to abuse food.

I only use sweeteners like sugar, honey, coconut sugar, date syrup, maple syrup, or the now hard-to-find coconut nectar. I cannot tolerate artificial sweeteners or sugar substitutes, so I never work with those. If you would like to use artificial sweeteners or sugar substitutes, then that's up to you. If you're using them to be able to eat more sweets on a daily basis to try to game the low-carb system, then I can assure you, you won't win. Our endocrine systems and bodies are wonders of nature and cannot be tricked. Instead, I gently invite you to try to give up sweet flavors for a while. If you do this, you will change your palate. Berries will taste sweet. Vanilla and heavy cream will satisfy your need for dessert decadence. It's an empowering place to be.

I include a sweets chapter in all the books I write because I've found that everyone who goes low carb eventually ends up eating sugar again. I want you all to have lower-sugar, grain-free versions of desserts that feel like celebratory treats.

Va bene, cuciniamo . . .

XOXO
Anna

ANTIPASTI

Italians bring local seasonal food to an art form. Antipasto, *which translates to "appetizer," or more literally "before pasta," is a course of foods that are easy to grab at the local farmers' market and are served on a small plate that everyone can fight over at the table. In this chapter, I've used almond flour and cheese to create cracker replicas, plus various dips and bites to tide you over until the next course. Since we're doing low carb, we're eliminating the bread dipped in olive oil. Instead, drizzle that olive oil on any of these dishes to give it some extra flair with a healthy fat.*

PROSCIUTTO-WRAPPED RICOTTA-STUFFED ARTICHOKE HEARTS

 YIELDS 20–24 BITES

IF YOU MAKE A LOT OF ITALIAN FOOD, YOU PROBABLY *have a package of prosciutto in the fridge as well as a can of artichoke hearts and Marcona almonds as pantry staples. It's easy to make homemade ricotta (or you can use high-quality store-bought ricotta) for a quick starter ready to whip up.*

1 (8-ounce) jar artichoke hearts in water, drained

1 cup full-fat ricotta cheese, homemade (page 35) or store-bought

20–24 Marcona almonds

3–4 ounces prosciutto slices, cut lengthwise into 1-inch strips

Olive oil, for drizzling

Balsamic vinegar, for drizzling

Trim the rough ends off the artichoke hearts and discard. Slice the artichoke hearts in half lengthwise. Place them cut side down on a paper towel to drain the excess water. Press them slightly to remove any additional water, then turn them cut side up.

Spoon a small dollop of ricotta cheese on each artichoke half, add a Marcona almond in the middle, then wrap a strip of prosciutto around it. If needed, hold everything together with a toothpick.

Heat a large nonstick sauté pan over medium-high heat. Toast the wrapped bites on all sides until the prosciutto is crispy, 2–3 minutes.

Transfer the bites to a serving platter and let them cool to room temperature. Drizzle with olive oil and balsamic vinegar and serve.

FAVA BEAN, RICOTTA, AND MINT

 SERVES 2–4

Salt and pepper

2 pounds fava beans, removed from their pods

3 tablespoons olive oil, plus more for drizzling

1 teaspoon minced lemon zest

Juice of ½ lemon (about 1 tablespoon)

1 teaspoon chopped fresh chives

1 tablespoon roughly chopped fresh mint leaves

1 cup full-fat ricotta cheese, homemade (page 35) or store-bought

THIS DISH IS QUINTESSENTIAL SPRING. BRIGHT AND *light, it's the perfect starter to get the appetite going. It's traditionally served atop bread for bruschetta or with pasta, but I like to serve it in individual ramekins or as a starter to share at the table.*

Bring a large pot of salted water to a boil. Blanch the fava beans for 2–3 minutes, or until they turn bright green and are slightly tender. Drain the fava beans and let cool enough to allow you to remove and discard the waxy skins.

In a small bowl, whisk together the olive oil, lemon zest, lemon juice, and chives. Season with salt and pepper. Fold in the fava beans and mint. Taste and season once more with salt and pepper if needed.

On a small serving dish or flat bowl, spread out the ricotta. Drizzle a bit of olive oil over it. Pour the fava bean mixture onto the ricotta cheese and serve.

FRIED BABY ARTICHOKES WITH LEMON CAPER AIOLI

 SERVES 2–4

IN CALIFORNIA, ARTICHOKE SEASON IS JUST DURING *April and May, so you have to grab baby artichokes when you see them. This once-a-year treat is worth all the peeling and chopping. And, of course, they're gone about 2 minutes after you serve them. Delicioso.*

Pro tip: Aioli is the Italian word for mayo. You are welcome to make homemade mayo (I have a recipe in my first cookbook, Eat Happy) *or use store-bought. When looking at labels, I try to find mayos that use mild olive oil, avocado oil, or MCT oil. I avoid mayonnaise made with seed oils such as soybean oil and canola oil.*

2 pounds baby artichokes

¼–½ cup olive oil

Salt and pepper

½ cup freshly grated parmesan cheese

1 tablespoon capers

1 cup mayonnaise

Juice of ½ lemon (about 1 tablespoon)

Slice the rough bottom stems off the artichokes and discard. Using your hands, peel off the outer leaves. Using a paring knife, peel and discard the outer bottom leaves from the stem. Cut off the rough tips of the leaves and discard so only the tender green artichoke heart and light green leaves remain. Cut the artichokes in half.

In a large, flat-bottomed sauté pan, heat ¼ cup of the olive oil over medium-high heat. Add as many artichokes as will fit comfortably without crowding and fry them for about 3 minutes per side, until browned and crispy. Transfer the artichokes to paper towels to drain. Fry the remaining artichokes in the same way, adding more oil as needed.

Put all the fried artichokes in a large bowl, season with salt and pepper, and toss with the fresh parmesan.

In a small bowl, crush the capers with the back of a wooden spoon. Whisk in the mayonnaise and lemon juice.

Serve the artichokes with the lemon caper mayonnaise for dipping.

EGGPLANT PARM BITES

 YIELDS 20–25 BITES

1–2 pounds baby/mini eggplants or thin Japanese eggplants, sliced into ¼-inch-thick disks

Salt and pepper

1 large egg

1 tablespoon heavy cream or coconut cream

1 cup almond flour or crushed pork rinds (such as Pork Panko)

1 teaspoon garlic powder

1 teaspoon onion powder

½ teaspoon dried basil

½ teaspoon dried oregano

⅓ cup olive oil, or more as needed

1 (26-ounce) jar Eat Happy Kitchen Tomato Basil Marinara *or* 2–3 cups Homemade Tomato Basil Marinara (page 30), heated

Small fresh basil leaves, for garnish

Freshly grated parmesan cheese, for garnish

IF YOU CAN FIND MINI EGGPLANTS OR THIN JAPANESE eggplants, you'll be able to create little bite-sized pieces. And if you can't find any eggplant that size, you can always substitute zucchini for the eggplant.

Line a rimmed baking sheet with paper towels. Place the eggplant slices in a single layer on the paper towels. Season with salt and pepper on both sides. Let the eggplant "sweat" for 10 minutes (the salt will draw beads of water out of the eggplant). Blot the eggplant dry with more paper towels.

In a small bowl, whisk together the egg and cream until mixed and pale yellow. In a medium bowl, whisk together the almond flour, garlic powder, onion powder, dried basil, and dried oregano.

Heat the olive oil in a large nonstick sauté pan over medium-high heat until shimmering. Do the sizzle test: Sprinkle a bit of the almond flour mix into the hot oil, and if it sizzles, the oil is hot enough for frying.

Dip the eggplant slices in the egg-cream mixture, then roll them in the almond flour to coat. Place one coated eggplant slice in the oil at the twelve o'clock position, then place additional slices clockwise in the pan. Cook for 2–3 minutes per side, until browned, then gently flip the eggplant slices starting at the twelve o'clock position and working your way around the pan clockwise. Cook the other side for 2–3 minutes, until brown. Transfer the slices to paper towels to drain. Fry the remaining slices in the same way, adding more oil as needed.

Place the eggplant slices on a platter. Dollop a teaspoon of marinara on each bite, flattening it a bit with the spoon. Garnish each bite with a basil leaf and a sprinkling of fresh parmesan.

ROCKFISH CRUDO

 SERVES 4

CRUDO MEANS "RAW," AND IT'S THE ITALIAN EQUIVA-
lent of sashimi, which is Japanese for "raw fish slices." Be
sure to buy sashimi-grade fish from the seafood depart-
ment of your grocery store or butcher. This recipe will
work well with nearly any white fish or tuna you can find.
Sharpen your knife to achieve that superthin, melt-in-
your-mouth crudo.

On a chilled serving plate, lay out the fish slices.
In a small bowl, whisk together the lime juice,
lemon juice, orange juice, and olive oil. Drizzle over the
fish slices. Season the fish with sea salt flakes, making
sure each piece gets some flakes. Scatter the cherry
tomatoes, radishes, and chives evenly around the
serving platter. Top with the red pepper flakes. Serve
immediately.

1 pound rockfish, halibut,
snapper, yellowtail, or alba-
core tuna, very thinly sliced,
kept cold

Juice of ½ lime (about 1 tablespoon)

Juice of ½ lemon (about 1 tablespoon)

Juice of ½ blood orange or regular
orange (about 2 tablespoons)

1 tablespoon olive oil

Sea salt flakes (I like Maldon)

¼ cup cherry tomatoes, quartered

2 radishes, thinly sliced

1 teaspoon minced fresh chives

¼ teaspoon red pepper flakes

SEARED CARPACCIO

 SERVES 4–6

1 (2-pound) beef tenderloin

Salt and pepper

2 tablespoons mayonnaise

Juice of ½ lemon (about 1 tablespoon), plus lemon wedges for
garnish

1 teaspoon Dijon mustard

1 teaspoon balsamic vinegar

1–2 cups arugula

Shaved parmesan cheese, for
garnish

1 tablespoon capers, for garnish

CARPACCIO IS WHISPER-THIN CUTS OF RAW BEEF
*tenderloin drizzled with a vinaigrette and garnished with
arugula, parmesan, and capers. It's basically an entire
meal when I make it. But you can make it and share. Shar-
ing is caring, after all.*

*I like to sear my beef tenderloin first, but if you're
pressed for time, the most important element is getting
that tenderloin in the freezer for 30 minutes to 2 hours first
to help you slice it thinner. Please use extra caution with
slicing, whether you use a knife, deli slicer, or mandoline.*

*Beef tenderloin is a longer, uncut filet mignon, which is
a pricey cut of meat. Since you are slicing this one so thinly,
you can try this recipe with a London broil to save some lira.*

*Fun piece of lore: Carpaccio is named after the Venetian
Renaissance painter Vittore Carpaccio (shout out, bro!) for
his use of reds and whites in his paintings.*

Season the beef tenderloin all over with salt and
pepper.

Heat a large, flat-bottomed sauté pan over high
heat. Add the tenderloin and sear for 1 minute per side.
Remove from the heat and let cool for a few minutes.
Wrap the tenderloin in plastic wrap or place in a freezer-
safe container and freeze for at least 30 minutes or up
to 2 hours. The tenderloin needs to be hard enough to
slice easily but not frozen solid.

Meanwhile, in a small bowl, whisk together the mayonnaise, lemon juice, mustard, and vinegar. Cover and
refrigerate until ready to serve.

Slice the tenderloin paper-thin, or as thin as possible, and arrange it on salad plates. Top the slices with
a handful of arugula, then drizzle with the dressing.
Garnish each plate with parmesan, capers, and lemon
wedges, then serve.

FRICO

 YIELDS 4–5 CHEESE DISKS

FRICO IS TRADITIONALLY PAN-FRIED CHEESE, ONION, *and potato, but we are eliminating the potato and adding bell pepper to maintain the shape. Fried cheese is popular in the low-carb world, but frico is way more fun than plain fried cheese, both to say and to eat.*

½ sweet onion, thinly sliced

½ red or orange bell pepper, cored and thinly sliced

1 cup shredded mozzarella cheese, divided

1 cup freshly grated parmesan cheese, divided

Eat Happy Kitchen Tomato Basil Marinara or Home-made Tomato Basil Marinara (page 30), heated, for dipping

Chopped fresh parsley, for garnish (optional)

Heat a large, flat-bottomed nonstick sauté pan over medium-high heat. Add the onion and cook until soft, 5–7 minutes. Remove the onion to a plate.

Reduce the heat to medium. In the same pan, add one-quarter each of the onion, bell pepper, mozzarella, and parmesan and shape the mixture into a disk. Cook until the cheese melts and gets bubbly, 2–3 minutes. Using a spatula, carefully transfer the frico to paper towels to drain and cool completely. Repeat with the remaining ingredients to make 3 more frico disks. If you like, garnish the frico with chopped parsley. Serve whole or break into chips and dip in marinara.

MORTADELLA DIP WITH HOMEMADE PARMESAN CHIPS

 YIELDS 1 CUP DIP AND 24 PARMESAN CHIPS

1 cup freshly grated parmesan cheese

8 ounces mortadella

3 tablespoons salted butter, at room temperature, cut into cubes

6 no-sugar-added cornichons or mini gherkins, finely chopped

Salt and pepper

Cut-up veggies, for serving

THIS RECIPE IS AN HOMAGE TO RENOWNED ITALIAN cookbook author Marcella Hazan, often referred to as the Italian JC. And by JC, I mean Julia Child.

If you can get a whole 8-ounce chunk of mortadella, then great. But if not, buy it sliced, then give it a few chops before putting it into the food processor.

Parmesan crisps are super easy to make, plus you can customize them by adding garlic powder or herbs. But they're also delicious plain as a cracker substitute.

Preheat the oven to 400 degrees F.

Divide the parmesan among the 24 cups of a nonstick mini-muffin tin. Bake until the cheese is bubbling, 10–12 minutes. Remove the tin from the oven and let cool until the cheese is crispy. Transfer the chips to paper towels to drain until ready to serve.

If the mortadella has casing, peel or cut that off and discard it. Cut the mortadella into 1-inch chunks. Put the mortadella and butter in a food processor and process until smooth. Remove the mixture from the food processor and fold in the cornichon pieces. Using a spatula, press the dip into a ramekin or small serving bowl. Cover and refrigerate for at least 1 hour.

Serve the chilled dip with the parmesan chips and veggies.

WHITE BEAN DIP

 YIELDS 1½ CUPS

WHILE I DON'T EAT A LOT OF BEANS ON A LOW-CARB *diet, I do love the occasional white bean dip or soup. White beans are a great protein option for vegetarians, and they are tasty enough to please the omnivores at the table. Make sure you rinse the canned beans until the cloudy liquid around them runs clear.*

Heat the oil in a small sauté pan over medium-low heat. Add the garlic and red pepper flakes and cook for 3–5 minutes, until fragrant. Remove the pan from the heat as soon as the garlic starts to brown and set aside. The garlic will continue to brown as it cools.

In a food processor or blender, combine the beans, salt, smoked paprika, garlic powder, onion powder, black pepper, and ¼ cup of the pine nuts and process until smooth. If needed, add water, 1 tablespoon at a time, to reach the desired consistency. Transfer the mixture to a serving bowl. Fold in the sun-dried tomatoes.

Drizzle the garlic–red pepper oil over the top, then the sun-dried tomato oil. Garnish with the remaining 1 tablespoon pine nuts and chopped parsley if desired and serve with the chips and cucumber slices.

¼ cup olive oil

2 garlic cloves, thinly sliced

¼ teaspoon red pepper flakes

1 (15–ounce) can great northern or cannellini beans, drained and rinsed

½ teaspoon salt

½ teaspoon smoked paprika

¼ teaspoon garlic powder

¼ teaspoon onion powder

¼ teaspoon black pepper

¼ cup plus 1 tablespoon toasted salted pine nuts, divided

1–3 tablespoons water

¼ cup sun-dried tomatoes in oil, finely chopped, plus 1 teaspoon oil

Chopped fresh parsley, for garnish (optional)

Sun-Dried Tomato and Almond Flour Chips (page 20) and sliced cucumber, for serving

SUN-DRIED TOMATO AND ALMOND FLOUR CHIPS

 YIELDS 20–25 CHIPS

1½ cups almond flour

1 large egg

½ teaspoon salt

½ teaspoon garlic powder

½ teaspoon dried oregano

1 tablespoon sun-dried tomatoes,
    finely chopped

THIS IS A DELICIOUS AND SIMPLE-TO-MAKE GRAIN-*free almond cracker. It's better to eat them within 24 hours so they're as fresh as possible, but they will get gobbled up by guests long before the party is over anyhow.*

Preheat the oven to 350 degrees F. Combine all the ingredients in a medium bowl and form into a dough ball.

Place a piece of parchment paper on your work surface. Place the dough ball on the parchment, then place another piece of parchment paper over the dough ball. Roll out the dough as thin as possible, about ¼ inch. Remove the top parchment and transfer the dough and bottom parchment to a rimmed baking sheet. Bake for 10–15 minutes, until toasted brown.

Remove from the oven and let cool, then break apart into chips and serve.

Pictured on page 18 with White Bean Dip

ANTIPASTI PLATTER

 SERVES 6–8

THIS ANTIPASTI PLATTER IS NOT SO MUCH A RECIPE, *but Italian charcuterie board goals. Gather your favorite ingredients and arrange them on a gorgeous cutting board. Mine was carved from olive wood by my late friend and olive oil proprietor Paul Cappelli. I cherish this board and use it the way he intended, by piling it high with copious amounts of meat, cheese, and olives to share with loved ones. If you want to keep your charcuterie board picture perfect, make sure you rub it with mineral oil every few months to preserve the wood.*

Salami, sliced

Prosciutto, sliced

Capocollo or bresaola, sliced

Pepper-coated hard salami, sliced or cubed

Variety of olives

Parmesan cheese, cut into chunks

Mini bell peppers stuffed with gorgonzola cheese

Cherry tomatoes, halved

Mini mozzarella cheese balls

Sun-dried tomatoes, chopped

Whole peperoncini

Canned or jarred artichoke hearts, halved

Olive oil, for drizzling

Fresh basil leaves, for garnish

Fresh rosemary sprigs, for garnish

Assemble all the ingredients except the olive oil and herbs on a charcuterie board or platter using your most artistic flair. Drizzle the parmesan cheese with olive oil and garnish the board with the basil and rosemary.

Pictured on chapter opener

MAKE YOUR OWN

I usually put the Make Your Own chapter further toward the back of my cookbooks to be used as a reference. However, so many of my recipes rely on homemade sauces, garnishes, tapenades, or dressings as important components, I moved this chapter to the front of the book. You will be referencing it often as you create from-scratch Italian classics. Once you have it down, you will be so glad you took the time to memorize how to knock out a fresh marinara or pesto at the drop of a hat.

Caponata, page 24

CAPONATA

 YIELDS 4–5 CUPS

1 large eggplant *or* 2 small eggplants, cut into 1-inch cubes

Salt and black pepper

2 tablespoons olive oil

1 sweet onion, roughly chopped

1 red bell pepper, cored and
roughly chopped

3 celery stalks, roughly chopped

3 garlic cloves, minced

1 (14–ounce) can no-sugar-
added diced tomatoes *or*
½ (26-ounce) jar Eat Happy
Kitchen Tomato Basil
Marinara

¼ cup chopped pitted Castelvetrano or other green olives

2 tablespoons drained capers

¼ cup balsamic vinegar

¼ cup white wine vinegar or white
balsamic vinegar

1 teaspoon red pepper flakes
(optional)

1 bay leaf

½ cup chopped fresh basil and/or
flat-leaf parsley

THE SICILIAN RATATOUILLE CAPONATA TAKES AGRO-
*dolce to the next level. Usually this recipe uses raisins
and honey to sweeten it, but we are going to omit those
ingredients. Not to worry, though. This dish is fabulous and
doesn't need sugar bombs. The two vinegars in this dish
reduce down to a very mellow sweetness that is unbeliev-
ably yummy.*

*I use green Castelvetrano olives for their milder brine
(plus they're Sicilian, just like this dish), but you are welcome to use pimiento-stuffed green olives or even black
kalamata olives.*

*Caponata can be a garnish, side dish, or condiment, and
its flavor gets better the longer you let it sit in the fridge.*

Preheat the oven to 350 degrees F. Line a rimmed
baking sheet with parchment paper.

Place the eggplant cubes on the prepared baking
sheet. Season with salt and black pepper. Let sit for 10
minutes to allow the eggplant to "sweat" (the salt will
draw beads of water out of the eggplant). Blot the eggplant dry with a paper towel. Roast for 20–25 minutes,
or until the eggplant is starting to brown. Set aside.

Meanwhile, in a Dutch oven or other large pot, heat
the olive oil over medium-high heat until shimmering.
Add the onion, bell pepper, and celery and cook, stirring frequently, until soft, 5–6 minutes. Add the garlic
and cook for 1–2 minutes, until fragrant. Add the tomatoes with their juices, bring to a low boil, and season
with salt and black pepper. Stir in the olives, capers,
balsamic vinegar, white wine vinegar, red pepper flakes
(if using), and bay leaf. Bring to a boil, then turn the
heat down to low and simmer for 10–15 minutes.

Stir in the eggplant cubes. Simmer for 5–8 more minutes to let the flavors marry. Remove from the heat and discard the bay leaf. Stir in the fresh herbs. Season once more with salt and black pepper if needed. Serve.

PESTO SAUCE

 YIELDS 1 CUP

I'VE BEEN MAKING PESTO SAUCE FOR SO LONG, IT'S *ingrained in my bones. If you want to be old school and use a mortar and pestle to grind the basil, you are my hero. I use a small food processor and usually make this recipe several times a week in the summer. Eat it fresh and in one sitting so that the basil doesn't oxidize. I use it atop tomatoes, soups, stews, grilled meats, or as a condiment alongside any Italian dish.*

2 cups fresh basil leaves

¼ cup raw or toasted pine nuts or walnuts

1 teaspoon minced garlic

⅓–½ cup olive oil

½ cup freshly grated parmesan cheese

Salt and pepper (optional)

Combine the basil, nuts, garlic, and ⅓ cup olive oil in a food processor or blender and pulse 3–5 times, until chopped. Scrape the sides with a spatula and pulse 3–5 more times. Scrape the sides again, add the parmesan, and pulse 3–4 more times, until the pesto is at your desired consistency. Add more olive oil if you'd like a smoother pesto, or leave it chunky for texture. Season with salt and pepper if desired and serve.

Pesto Sauce, recipe page 27

HOMEMADE TOMATO BASIL MARINARA

 YIELDS 2½ CUPS

1 tablespoon olive oil

1 teaspoon minced garlic

7–10 fresh basil leaves, chopped

2 (14–ounce) cans no-sugar-added diced tomatoes

3 ounces (6 tablespoons) tomato paste

1 teaspoon salt

1 teaspoon salted butter or additional olive oil (optional)

THIS IS MY OG MARINARA RECIPE THAT I'VE BEEN *making for 25 years from scratch. If you can't find Eat Happy Kitchen marinara near you, make it at home from this recipe, and you won't be disappointed.*

Around the time that my family came over from Italy, the canned tomatoes available were so harshly acidic that it became common practice to add a pinch of sugar or brown sugar when making sauce. This practice was a move out of necessity but has become canon in a lot of Italian American households. However, we don't need to add a pinch of sugar anymore to cut acid. First, we have much nicer canned tomatoes and paste available to us. Just make sure you check the ingredient label for no sugar added. Second, there's a trick at the end of the recipe to add butter or more olive oil to help cut the acid, which is something I suggest trying if you have a kid who finds red sauce too tangy.

You can make this marinara (or any of the following red sauces) on the fly for any number of recipes in this book and, of course, the longer it simmers, the better it gets. But if you want to order a case from my website, I'll pay for the shipping.

Heat the olive oil in a large saucepan over medium-high heat. Add the garlic and basil and cook for 1–2 minutes, until fragrant. Add the tomatoes with their juices, tomato paste, and salt and stir to combine. Bring to a boil, then reduce the heat and simmer for 10–15 minutes. If desired, add a pat of butter or another drizzle of olive oil to the finished marinara to cut the acidity. Serve immediately or store in an airtight container in the fridge for up to 10 days.

ARRABBIATA SPICY MARINARA

 YIELDS 2½ CUPS

ARRABBIATA MEANS "ANGRY." TYPICALLY, THIS IS A
*spicy red sauce, and if we're going to make it authentically,
we add pancetta (unsmoked Italian bacon). You can keep
this sauce vegetarian by omitting the pancetta, and it's
still plenty spicy.*

*I love Calabrian peppers in my arrabbiata; however, it's
hard to find these peppers packed in anything but sunflower oil. So I use dried Calabrian pepper flakes, which
are easy to find in Italian markets or online.*

*And of course, over at Eat Happy Kitchen, we make a
vegetarian arrabbiata sauce that's out of this world.*

1 tablespoon olive oil

⅓ cup diced pancetta

1 teaspoon Calabrian pepper
flakes or regular red pepper
flakes

1 teaspoon minced garlic

7–10 fresh basil leaves, chopped

2 (14–ounce) cans no-sugar-added
diced tomatoes

3 ounces (6 tablespoons) tomato
paste

1 teaspoon salt

Heat the olive oil in a large saucepan over medium-
high heat. Add the pancetta and cook until the fat
renders and the pancetta is crispy, 3–4 minutes. Add
the pepper flakes, garlic, and basil and cook for 1–2
minutes, until fragrant. Stir in the tomatoes with their
juices, tomato paste, and salt and stir to combine. Bring
to a boil, then reduce the heat and simmer for 15–20
minutes. Serve immediately or store in an airtight container in the fridge for up to 10 days.

PUTTANESCA SAUCE

 YIELDS 2½ CUPS

1 tablespoon olive oil

½ medium onion, diced

1 teaspoon minced garlic

¾ cup pitted black olives, chopped

2 tablespoons drained capers

½ teaspoon onion powder

½ teaspoon red pepper flakes

1 teaspoon salt, divided, plus more for seasoning

7–10 fresh basil leaves, chopped

1 teaspoon chopped fresh oregano leaves, plus more for garnish

2 (14–ounce) cans no-sugar-added diced tomatoes, 1 can pureed in a blender

3 ounces (6 tablespoons) tomato paste

½ teaspoon black pepper, plus more for seasoning

I CALL PUTTANESCA MY HEARTY TOMATO STEW. IT *takes a marinara red sauce base and adds capers, black olives, onion, and oregano, plus red pepper flakes for extra heat at the end. A puttanesca sauce traditionally uses anchovies or anchovy paste as the umami flavor base, but I know my American peeps, and they would prefer to keep the anchovies out of it. So instead of lecturing my Eat Happy audience, lovingly called Happies, on the glorious-ness of anchovies, I created this anchovy-free version of puttanesca sauce, which is just as delicious, if not more so.*

Heat the olive oil in a large saucepan over medium-high heat. Add the onion and garlic and cook until soft, 3–4 minutes. Add the olives, capers, onion powder, red pepper flakes, ½ teaspoon of the salt, basil, and oregano and cook, stirring occasionally, for 2–3 minutes, until fragrant. Stir in the tomatoes with their juices, tomato paste, remaining ½ teaspoon salt, and black pepper. Bring to a boil, then turn the heat down and simmer for 15–20 minutes. Season with additional salt and black pepper, if needed. Serve immediately or store in an airtight container in the fridge for up to 10 days.

AGRODOLCE SAUCE

 YIELDS 1 CUP

AGRODOLCE TRANSLATES TO "SOUR-SWEET," AND *it's an incredible topping for any seafood dish, whether baked or grilled, white fish or pan-seared shellfish. If you remember to make the agrodolce sauce a couple of days before your meal, the flavors will marry into the perfect blend of sweet and sour, with a bit of a kick from Calabrian pepper flakes.*

⅓ cup dried cherries, chopped

¼ cup sherry vinegar

⅓ cup olive oil

¼ cup raw almonds, chopped

2 shallots, thinly sliced into rings

½ teaspoon Calabrian pepper flakes

1 teaspoon salt

In a small bowl, soak the dried cherries in the sherry vinegar and set aside.

Heat the olive oil in a large sauté pan over medium heat. Add the almonds and toast until they just start to turn golden brown and become fragrant, 2–3 minutes. Remove the pan from the heat and let cool.

Add the shallots and Calabrian pepper flakes to the bowl with the soaking cherries. Add the cooled nuts and oil. Stir in the salt. Cover the bowl and refrigerate for at least 8 hours. Bring the agrodolce sauce to room temperature before serving.

ALFREDO SAUCE

 YIELDS 1½ CUPS

4 tablespoons salted butter

1 garlic clove, minced

½ teaspoon finely chopped fresh
oregano leaves

1 cup heavy cream

Salt and pepper

1 cup freshly grated parmesan
cheese, plus more for garnish

THE ZUCCHINI NOODLES ALFREDO RECIPE (PAGE 55)
*is in the Primi Piatti chapter, but I wanted the sauce to
be a standalone recipe here so you can make it anytime
you want to serve with veggies, chicken, or fish. It's quick
to cook, flavorful, and downright comforting. You can also
combine Alfredo with a marinara and make a damn fine
pink sauce.*

Heat the butter in a large, flat-bottomed sauté pan
over medium-high heat until it has melted and
is starting to bubble. Add the garlic and oregano and
stir for 1 minute. Add the cream and bring to a boil,
then turn the heat down to medium. Season the sauce
with salt and pepper and let it simmer for 5–7 minutes,
until thickened. Make sure to stir every 15–20 seconds
to prevent a skin from forming on the surface of the
sauce. Add the parmesan and stir until it's melted and
incorporated. Serve immediately, topped with more
parmesan.

HOMEMADE RICOTTA CHEESE

 YIELDS 1 CUP

ONCE YOU MAKE HOMEMADE RICOTTA, YOU WILL
*never go back to store-bought. I know that's a strong
claim, but, dang, it's so good and simple to make. Get a
nice cheesecloth from a kitchen supply store or online so
you can use it several times before discarding (rinsing well
between each use).*

4 cups whole milk

½ cup heavy cream

½ teaspoon salt

Juice of 1 lemon (about 2 tablespoons)

In a medium saucepan, bring the milk, cream, and salt to a boil over medium-high heat, stirring with a wooden spoon so a skin doesn't form along the sides of the pot. Once it comes to a boil, add the lemon juice. Turn the heat down to low and simmer, stirring constantly. The mixture will begin to curdle after 3–4 minutes. The curds will look quite tiny and then clump only slightly more.

Set a strainer over a large bowl and line the strainer with fine-mesh cheesecloth. Pour the milk mixture into the strainer. The liquid will strain through, and the ricotta will form out of the curds left in the cheese-cloth. Let the cheese curd mixture strain for no longer than 5–10 minutes to prevent the ricotta from getting too dry. Use the ricotta right away, or transfer it to an airtight container and refrigerate for up to 7 days.

OLIVE TAPENADE

 YIELDS 2½ CUPS

TRADITIONAL TAPENADE IS FANTASTIC AS A DIP OR A *portion of a charcuterie board. You can also rub it on meats before you grill or roast them. Traditional olive tapenade uses anchovy filets, but I've taken to anchovy paste, as it has the perfect smooth texture to complement the tapenade texture.*

⅓ cup raw pine nuts

2 cups pitted kalamata olives

2 tablespoons drained and rinsed capers

2 tablespoons olive oil

1 tablespoon anchovy paste (optional)

1 teaspoon lemon juice

½ teaspoon minced garlic

Sun-Dried Tomato and Almond Flour Chips (page 20), for serving

In a food processor, blend the pine nuts until they turn into a nut butter, about 30–45 seconds. Add the olives, capers, olive oil, anchovy paste (if using), lemon juice, and garlic and pulse about 10 times, until everything is finely chopped with a chunky paste consistency, scraping the sides of the food processor as needed.

Transfer the tapenade to an airtight container and refrigerate overnight to let the flavors marry. Bring it to room temperature before serving with Sundried Tomato and Almond Pita Chips.

GIARDINIERA OLIVE SALAD

 YIELDS 5¼ CUPS

VEGETABLES

1 cup cauliflower "rice"

3–4 celery stalks, cut into ½-inch
    pieces (about 1 cup)

2–3 carrots, cut into ½-inch
    pieces (about 1 cup)

1 cup sliced pimiento-stuffed
    green olives

½ cup chopped radishes

¼ cup drained capers

2 cups water

2 tablespoons salt

BRINE

1 cup water

½ cup white vinegar

¼ cup apple cider vinegar

¼ cup red wine vinegar

2 teaspoons salt

FOR THE JARS

1 teaspoon dried oregano

½ teaspoon black peppercorns

½ teaspoon red pepper flakes

½ teaspoon coriander seeds

½ teaspoon mustard seeds

¼ teaspoon celery seeds

2 garlic cloves, halved

2 tablespoons olive oil

THIS DELICIOUS VEGGIE AND OLIVE SALAD IS A PER-
fect pickled garnish, traditionally served on sandwiches
(the famous muffuletta) or alongside meats and veggies.
It's a process to pickle the veggies, so give this one some
time.

Combine the cauliflower rice, celery, carrots, olives, radishes, and capers in a large glass bowl. Add the water and salt, stir, and let sit in the fridge for 8 hours or overnight. In the morning, drain the veggies in a strainer and rinse well.

Combine all the brine ingredients in a small saucepan and bring to a boil.

While the brine comes to a boil, divide the oregano, peppercorns, red pepper flakes, coriander seeds, mustard seeds, and celery seeds between two pint-size mason jars. Divide the drained veggies between the jars, pressing to pack them in. Place 2 garlic halves in each jar atop the veggies. Pour enough hot brine into each jar to cover the veggies. (Discard any excess brine.) Pour 1 tablespoon olive oil into each jar. Wipe any spilled liquid or oil off the outside of the jars, then close tightly. Let the jars sit in a cool, dry place for 2 days before serving, then move the jars to the fridge, where they will keep for up to 2 weeks.

THE DRESSING TRIUMVIRATE

THESE THREE DRESSING RECIPES WILL COVER ALMOST ALL YOUR NEEDS. YOU CAN USE *them as salad dressings, marinades, or even dipping sauces. All three dressings require high-quality ingredients, so don't skimp on the olive oil, vinegars, or mayo. You could even make home-made mayo (ahem—aioli) as the base of your Caesar, if you don't care for store-bought mayo.*

A note about vinaigrettes (oil-and-vinegar dressings): Never forget the almighty 3:1 ratio (3 parts oil to 1 part vinegar). If you need to increase quantities, maintain that 3:1 ratio and you'll be in good shape. You can always add seasonings and extra ingredients to taste. That's why we love the versatility of vinaigrettes.

You'll find that the balsamic and Italian dressings are similar. That's by design. Because they are similar, we can swap out vinegar flavor profiles for variety.

Traditional Caesar dressing uses anchovies or anchovy paste (which, trust me, is a wonderful thing), but I'm making anchovy paste optional here, so you can omit it if there's a fish allergy or if you can't obtain anchovy paste.

BALSAMIC DRESSING

 YIELDS SCANT ½ CUP

⅓ cup olive oil

1 tablespoon balsamic vinegar

1 tablespoon red wine vinegar

2 teaspoons Dijon mustard

¼ teaspoon garlic powder

¼ teaspoon onion powder

¼ teaspoon dried basil

¼ teaspoon dried oregano

¼ teaspoon salt

¼ teaspoon pepper

In a small bowl, whisk all the ingredients together, then serve.

ITALIAN DRESSING

 YIELDS SCANT ½ CUP

6 tablespoons olive oil

2 tablespoons white balsamic or white wine vinegar

¼ teaspoon garlic powder

¼ teaspoon onion powder

¼ teaspoon dried basil

¼ teaspoon dried oregano

⅛ teaspoon salt

⅛ teaspoon pepper

In a small bowl, whisk all the ingredients together, then serve.

CAESAR DRESSING

 YIELDS SCANT ½ CUP

1 teaspoon minced garlic

3 tablespoons mayonnaise

1 tablespoon Dijon mustard

Juice of ½ lemon (about 1 tablespoon)

1 teaspoon balsamic vinegar

¼ teaspoon Worcestershire sauce

¼ teaspoon hot sauce

¼ cup freshly grated parmesan cheese

2 teaspoons anchovy paste (optional)

½ teaspoon salt, or more to taste

¼ teaspoon pepper, or more to taste

In a small bowl, use a fork to mash the garlic to a paste. Whisk in the mayonnaise, mustard, lemon juice, balsamic vinegar, Worcestershire sauce, and hot sauce. Then whisk in the parmesan, anchovy paste (if using), salt, and pepper. Taste the dressing and add more salt and pepper, if desired.

PRIMI PIATTI

Primi piatti *means "first courses," and it traditionally refers to the pasta or rice course. In this chapter I maintain the integrity of classic Italian dishes but use various veggies to substitute for the pasta or risotto. The tail end of this chapter is where you'll find three different low-carb pizza crusts and a calzone recipe best eaten with a knife and fork. All are delicious lower-carb options to get your pizza pie fix.*

Spaghetti Squash Amatriciana (and alla Gricia variation), page 58

WILD MUSHROOM CAULIFLOWER "RISOTTO"

 SERVES 2–3

THIS IS THE FIRST OF THREE RECIPES THAT SUBSTI-
*tute cauliflower grated into small pieces for the traditional
arborio rice that goes into risotto. Because we are remov-
ing the starch of the rice from these recipes, we will use
less liquid than we would with a traditional risotto. But
the flavor is all there. When you master the technique of a
low-carb risotto, you can add veggies, cheeses, herbs, and
meats for all kinds of possibilities.*

1 cup dried wild mushrooms

1 cup boiling water

2 tablespoons olive oil

1 medium sweet onion, finely
chopped

1 cup thinly sliced cremini or
baby portobello mushrooms

Salt and pepper

2 cups cauliflower "rice"

½ teaspoon garlic powder

½ teaspoon onion powder

1 tablespoon white wine vinegar

½ teaspoon fresh thyme leaves

½ teaspoon chopped fresh sage
leaves

½ teaspoon chopped fresh
oregano leaves

2 tablespoons cream cheese or
crème fraîche

½ cup freshly grated parmesan
cheese, plus more for garnish

Put the dried mushrooms in a small bowl, add the
boiling water, and set aside to soften for 20–30
minutes. Remove the mushrooms, reserving the soaking liquid, and finely chop them.

In a large, flat-bottomed nonstick sauté pan, heat
the olive oil over medium-high heat until shimmering. Add the onion and cook for 6–8 minutes, until
soft and translucent. Add the chopped reconstituted
mushrooms and sliced fresh mushrooms, season well
with salt and pepper, and cook for 3–4 minutes, until
softened.

Add the cauliflower, toss to coat, and cook for
2–3 minutes. Stir in the garlic powder, onion powder,
and 1 teaspoon salt. Add the vinegar and let sizzle for
2–3 minutes. Pour in the reserved mushroom liquid and
bring to a boil, then turn the heat down to a simmer. Season well with salt and pepper, stir in the thyme, sage, and
oregano, and simmer for 7–9 minutes, until the cauliflower is cooked but not mushy, stirring occasionally.

Remove the pan from the heat and fold in the cream
cheese and parmesan. Let stand for 3–5 minutes, then
serve with additional parmesan.

PRIMAVERA CAULIFLOWER "RISOTTO"

 SERVES 2–3

2 tablespoons salted butter

1 onion, finely chopped

1 garlic clove, minced

Salt and pepper

1 cup heavy cream

2 cups cauliflower "rice"

1 cup (1-inch) asparagus pieces

½ cup fresh or thawed frozen peas

1 cup freshly grated parmesan
    cheese

PRIMAVERA MEANS "SPRING" IN ITALIAN, AND THIS *recipe earns its title by using asparagus and peas, in season in the spring. However, you can use this recipe as a base for any low-carb vegetable "risotto" no matter what veggie season you're in.*

Melt the butter in a large, flat-bottomed sauté pan over medium-high heat. Add the onion and cook until soft, 3–4 minutes. Add the garlic and cook for 1–2 minutes, until fragrant. Season well with salt and pepper. Add the cream, cauliflower, and asparagus and bring to a boil. Reduce the heat to a simmer, cover, and simmer for 6–8 minutes. Stir in the peas, then stir in the parmesan. Season well with salt and pepper, cover the pan again, and cook for an additional 2–3 minutes. Season once more with salt and pepper if needed and serve.

LEMON MINT CAULIFLOWER "RISOTTO"

 SERVES 2–3

2 tablespoons olive oil

1 sweet onion, diced

1 garlic clove, minced

2 cups cauliflower "rice"

Salt and pepper

¼ cup chicken broth

¼ cup heavy cream

2 tablespoons grated lemon zest

Juice of 1 lemon (about 2 tablespoons)

½ cup chopped fresh mint leaves

THIS IS A WONDERFUL SPRING OR SUMMER SIDE *dish with grilled chicken, steak, or salmon. Lemon and cream together make one of my favorite comfort food taste sensations.*

Heat the olive oil in a large, flat-bottomed sauté pan over medium-high heat. Add the onion and cook until soft, 3–4 minutes. Add the garlic and cook for 1–2 minutes, until fragrant. Add the cauliflower, season well with salt and pepper, and cook for 3–4 minutes. Add the broth, cream, lemon zest, and lemon juice. Stir and cook for 3–4 minutes, until the cauliflower is cooked but not mushy. Turn off the heat and stir in the mint leaves. Serve immediately.

CAULIFLOWER GNOCCHI

 SERVES 2

THE BIGGEST TIP I CAN GIVE FOR THIS RECIPE IS TO *make sure you roll out and press the cooked cauliflower rice so it is as dry as possible before forming it into the gnocchi. When you add the fresh pesto to the cauliflower gnocchi, make sure to gently spoon it on top so as not to damage the gnocchi.*

For the pesto sauce: Combine the basil, nuts, garlic, and ⅓ cup olive oil in a food processor or blender and pulse 3–5 times, until chopped. Scrape the sides with a spatula and pulse 3–5 more times. Scrape the sides again, add the parmesan, and pulse 3–4 more times, until the pesto is at your desired consistency. Add more olive oil if you'd like a smoother pesto, or leave it chunky for texture. Season with salt and pepper if desired.

For the gnocchi: Put the cauliflower rice in a large microwave-safe bowl and microwave on high for 3 minutes. Divide the cauliflower evenly between two clean kitchen towels and spread it all out. Press the excess water out of the cauliflower, let it stand for 10 minutes, then press some more. Transfer the cauliflower to a medium bowl. Add the mozzarella, parmesan, almond flour, and salt. Using a fork, stir in the egg yolks one at a time until they are thoroughly mixed. Place the bowl, uncovered, in the fridge for 1 hour.

Preheat the oven to 400 degrees F. Line a rimmed baking sheet with parchment paper, then spray it with olive oil spray.

Form the cauliflower mixture into gnocchi about 1 inch wide and 1½ inches long. Place them on the prepared baking sheet. Bake on the bottom rack of the oven for 10 minutes. Let stand for 5–10 minutes, then serve with the pesto gently spooned over the top.

PESTO SAUCE

2 cups fresh basil leaves

¼ cup raw or toasted pine nuts or walnuts

1 teaspoon minced garlic

⅓–½ cup olive oil

½ cup freshly grated parmesan cheese

Salt and pepper (optional)

GNOCCHI

2 cups cauliflower "rice"

½ (8-ounce) ball fresh mozzarella cheese, excess water pressed out, shredded (about ½ cup)

½ cup freshly grated parmesan cheese

¼ cup almond flour

1 teaspoon salt

2 large egg yolks

Olive oil spray

Pictured on pages 50–51

Cauliflower Gnocchi, recipe page 49

ZUCCHINI NOODLES BOLOGNESE

 SERVES 2–4

4 tablespoons olive oil, divided

1 medium onion, finely diced

1 medium carrot or 6 baby carrots, finely diced

1 celery stalk, finely diced

2 ounces pancetta, chopped

1 pound ground beef

2 large garlic cloves, chopped

1 teaspoon salted butter

2 teaspoons salt

½ teaspoon pepper

½ teaspoon garlic powder

½ teaspoon onion powder

1 (26-ounce) jar Eat Happy Kitchen Marinara *or* 3 cups Homemade Tomato Basil Marinara (page 30)

½ cup chicken broth

½ teaspoon dried thyme

1 bay leaf

Salt and pepper

¼ cup half-and-half

3–4 zucchini

Shaved parmesan cheese, for serving

I KNOW AT FIRST GLANCE, IT SEEMS BIZARRE TO *write an Italian food book with no pasta. But here we are. And guess what? We will make some dishes that are so delicious you won't even miss the pasta.*

I'm trying to help the folks who can no longer tolerate pasta with any regularity (whether from high blood sugar or too much gluten), so I've relied on zucchini noodles, spaghetti squash noodles, and hearts of palm noodles to substitute for pasta. These are the three vegetable solutions that I've found to work the best and hold up to our favorite Italian sauces.

The traditional Bolognese sauce is slow-cooked, tomato-based goodness. You can eat it on its own or combine it with zucchini noodles as in the recipe here. We want the noodle to be able to sustain the sauce, and Bolognese is perfect for spiralized zucchini noodles.

I've found that a vegetable spiralizer is a good investment, since spiralizing your own zucchini noodles is much less expensive than buying them pre-spiralized at the store. I spent $30 on my Paderno spiralizer eleven years ago, and it's still going strong. You can get a handheld device or even an attachment for your food processor, whatever works for you.

Heat 1 tablespoon of the olive oil in a Dutch oven or other large pot over medium heat until shimmering. Add the onion, carrot, celery, and pancetta and cook, stirring occasionally, until the pancetta is crispy and the vegetables are softened but not browned, 6–8 minutes. Transfer the mixture to a large bowl, leaving the rendered pancetta fat in the pot.

Add the remaining 3 tablespoons olive oil to the pot and turn the heat up to medium-high. Add the ground beef and cook until it's just barely pink, about 5 minutes. Return the vegetable mixture to the pot, along with the garlic, butter, salt, pepper, garlic powder, and onion powder, turn the heat up to high, and cook until fragrant, about 1 minute.

Stir in the marinara, broth, thyme, and bay leaf. Bring to a boil, then cover partially, reduce the heat to medium-low, and cook for 30 minutes. Discard the bay leaf. Stir in the half-and-half until well blended. Taste the sauce and season with additional salt and pepper if needed.

While the sauce is cooking, line a rimmed baking sheet with paper towels. Spiralize the zucchini into noodles. Spread out the zucchini noodles on the paper towels, season with salt, and let the zucchini noodles "sweat" for 10–15 minutes (the salt will draw beads of water out of the zucchini). Blot the zucchini noodles dry with a paper towel.

Add the zucchini noodles to the simmering sauce, tossing to coat. Cover and simmer for 10–12 minutes, or until the noodles are at the desired firmness. Season with additional salt and pepper if needed. Serve topped with fresh parmesan.

ZUCCHINI NOODLES ALFREDO

 SERVES 4

YOU WILL NEVER BE AT A LOSS FOR A QUICK LUNCH *or dinner with this recipe in your toolbelt. While the Alfredo Sauce recipe (page 34) is also in the Make Your Own chapter, I'm including it again here so you don't have to flip back and forth in the book (also because it is just so darn good with zucchini noodles). Feel free to add a protein of your choice or eat it on its own.*

4 zucchini

Salt and pepper

4 tablespoons salted butter

1 garlic clove, minced

½ teaspoon finely chopped fresh oregano leaves

1 cup heavy cream

1 cup freshly grated parmesan cheese, plus more for garnish

1 tablespoon chopped fresh flat-leaf parsley, for garnish

Line a rimmed baking sheet with paper towels. Spiralize the zucchini into noodles. Spread out the noodles on the paper towels, season with salt, and let the zucchini noodles "sweat" for 10–15 minutes (the salt will draw beads of water out of the zucchini) to release excess water while you prepare the sauce.

Heat the butter in a large, flat-bottomed sauté pan over medium-high heat until it has melted and is starting to bubble. Add the garlic and oregano and stir for 1 minute. Add the cream and bring to a boil, then turn the heat down to medium. Season the sauce with salt and pepper and let it simmer for 5–7 minutes, until thickened. Make sure to stir every 15–20 seconds to prevent a skin from forming on the surface of the sauce. Add the parmesan and stir until it's melted and incorporated.

Blot the zucchini noodles dry with a paper towel.

In another large, nonstick sauté pan, cook the zucchini noodles over medium-high heat, tossing gently, for 4–5 minutes, until they have slightly softened. Season the noodles with salt and pepper. Transfer the noodles to the sauce and toss until the noodles are covered. Serve immediately, topped with fresh parmesan and chopped parsley.

ZUCCHINI NOODLES WITH WALNUT SAGE SAUCE

 SERVES 3–4

2–3 zucchini

Salt and pepper

1½ cups shelled walnut halves

2 cups heavy cream

2 garlic cloves, thinly sliced

1 tablespoon minced fresh sage
leaves, plus more for garnish

⅓ cup freshly grated parmesan
cheese, plus more for garnish

THIS RECIPE WOULD ALSO BE GOOD WITH SHREDDED *chicken, but it's filling on its own. Walnut sauce is a traditional Italian sauce, and often prepared when meats or fresh vegetables aren't available. The result is a nutty, decadent alternative to Alfredo.*

Preheat the oven to 350 degrees F. Line a rimmed baking sheet with paper towels. Spiralize the zucchini into noodles. Spread out the noodles on the paper towels, season with salt, and let the zucchini noodles "sweat" for 10–15 minutes (the salt will draw beads of water out of the zucchini). Blot the zucchini noodles dry with a paper towel.

Meanwhile, place the walnut halves on a rimmed baking sheet and toast in the oven for 10–12 minutes, until the walnuts become fragrant and start to brown. Remove them from the oven and chop the walnuts or pulse them in a mini food processor until they're finely chopped.

In a large, flat-bottomed sauté pan, heat the cream over medium heat. Add the garlic and cook until fragrant, 2–3 minutes. Add the sage, toasted walnut pieces, and 1 teaspoon salt. Bring to a low boil and let the sauce simmer for 8–10 minutes, being careful not to let the cream scald or stick to the sides of the pan. Season with pepper.

Add the zucchini noodles to the cream sauce, tossing to coat. Cook for 8–10 minutes, or until the zucchini noodles are tender but not overcooked. Serve garnished with fresh parmesan and chopped sage.

SPAGHETTI SQUASH AMATRICIANA
(and alla Gricia variation)

 SERVES 2

1 spaghetti squash

Salt and pepper

1 tablespoon olive oil

½ cup chopped guanciale or
pancetta

½ sweet onion, thinly sliced

3 tablespoons white wine vinegar
or white balsamic vinegar

1½ cups canned diced no-sugar-
added tomatoes or Home-
made Tomato Basil Marinara
(page 30)

¼ cup grated pecorino romano
cheese, plus more for garnish

Chopped fresh basil leaves, for
garnish

THE FOUR FAMOUS ROMAN PASTA DISHES ARE ALL *variations on one another: alla carbonara, alla gricia, all'amatriciana, and cacio e pepe. I use spaghetti squash for amatriciana and carbonara, plus I provide a variation in this recipe to make the delicious gricia (Greek-style) version. For the classic Roman favorite cacio e pepe, see the Verdure e Contorni chapter for my Asparagus Cacio e Pepe (page 154).*

Guanciale is at the heart of amatriciana, carbonara, and gricia. It is cured pork jowl, which is rich, flavorful, and decadent. If you cannot find guanciale in your local market, you can substitute pancetta or bacon. In fact, I use bacon in my carbonara recipe that follows, and it is pure bliss.

Preheat the oven to 350 degrees F. Microwave the spaghetti squash for 2 minutes on high. Slice the squash in half lengthwise, then scrape out and discard the seeds. Place the squash halves cut side down on a rimmed baking sheet. Roast for 35–40 minutes, until the squash is soft. The outside shell should easily cave in when pressed. Remove the sheet from the oven, flip over the squash halves, and let them cool enough to be able to use a fork to scrape the "spaghetti" strands into a bowl. Discard the squash shells. Season the strands with salt and pepper.

Heat the olive oil in a large, flat-bottomed nonstick sauté pan over medium-high heat until shimmering. Add the guanciale and let the fat render until it starts to brown, 3–4 minutes. Add the onion and cook until softened, 3–4 minutes. Add the vinegar and stir to make sure any bits stuck on the bottom of the pan are loosened. Pour in the tomatoes with their juices and season with salt and pepper. Bring to a boil, then reduce the heat and simmer for 8–10 minutes.

Remove the pan from the heat and stir in the pecorino. Fold in the spaghetti squash strands and toss until mixed. Serve topped with chopped basil and additional grated pecorino.

Pictured on page 42

ALLA GRICIA VARIATION

To make spaghetti squash alla gricia, follow the recipe above but omit the tomato sauce. Simply cook the guanciale or pancetta in olive oil, toss with the spaghetti squash strands, and garnish with freshly grated parmesan or pecorino cheese.

SPAGHETTI SQUASH CARBONARA

 SERVES 2 AS A MAIN COURSE OR 4 AS A SIDE DISH

CARBONARA IS ONE OF THE FOUR FAMOUS ROMAN *pasta dishes (along with gricia, amatriciana, and cacio e pepe). As noted in my Spaghetti Squash Amatriciana recipe (page 58), spaghetti squash is my top pasta replacement for certain sauces.*

While guanciale (cured pork jowl) is the traditional ingredient for carbonara, here I use bacon—you can swap in bacon or pancetta for guanciale in many recipes, and here I like the meatier bite that bacon brings.

---

1 spaghetti squash

Salt and pepper

1 tablespoon olive oil

4 slices thick-cut bacon, halved lengthwise and cut crosswise into ½-inch pieces

1 teaspoon minced garlic

1 large egg plus 3 large egg yolks

1 cup freshly grated parmesan cheese

1 tablespoon chopped fresh flat-leaf parsley, for garnish

Preheat the oven to 350 degrees F. Microwave the spaghetti squash for 2 minutes on high. Slice the squash in half lengthwise, then scrape out and discard the seeds. Place the squash halves cut side down on a rimmed baking sheet. Roast for 35—40 minutes, until the squash is soft. The outside shell should easily cave in when pressed. Remove the sheet from the oven, flip over the squash halves, and let them cool enough to be able to use a fork to scrape the "spaghetti" strands into a bowl. Discard the squash shells. Season the strands with salt and pepper.

Heat the olive oil in a large, flat-bottomed sauté pan over medium-high heat. Add the bacon pieces and cook until almost cooked through and crispy, 6–7 minutes. Add the garlic and cook for 1–2 minutes, until fragrant. Add the spaghetti squash strands and toss well to combine and heat through. Season with salt and pepper.

In a medium bowl, whisk together the egg, egg yolks, and parmesan. When the spaghetti squash mixture is nice and hot, turn off the burner and immediately add the parmesan-egg mixture, tossing to coat evenly. The heat from the spaghetti squash will cook the eggs into a smooth, creamy sauce as you mix them together. Garnish with the parsley and serve immediately.

LINGUINE WITH CLAMS

 SERVES 2

3 tablespoons olive oil

2 shallots, finely chopped

2 garlic cloves, minced

½ cup dry white wine (I prefer a sauvignon blanc, but you can also use any non-oaky chardonnay.)

2 pounds littleneck clams, cleaned thoroughly, any open clams discarded

8 ounces hearts of palm linguine (I like Palmini), rinsed and drained

Salt and pepper

Juice of ½ lemon (about 1 tablespoon)

1–2 tablespoons salted butter

¼ cup chopped fresh flat-leaf parsley

THE INNOVATION OF NOODLES MADE FROM HEARTS *of palm was a pretty great thing for us low-carbers. Since there's more of a vinegar flavor profile to these noodles, I find that they go well with garlic- and white wine–based sauces or traditional marinara. I use Palmini, but there are also some good private-label store brands you can try.*

In a large, flat-bottomed sauté pan, heat the olive oil over medium-high heat until shimmering. Add the shallots and cook for 1–2 minutes, until soft, then add the garlic and cook for 1 minute. Add the wine and bring to a boil. Add the clams, then cover and let them steam for 5–6 minutes, or until the clams have opened. Discard any clams that haven't opened. Add the noodles, season with salt and pepper, and toss well. Add the lemon juice, butter, and parsley, toss again, and cook for 1–2 more minutes. Serve immediately.

DAIRY-FREE SHRIMP SCAMPI

 SERVES 2

YOU CAN MAKE THIS RECIPE DAIRY-FULL BY SWITCH-
ing out the dairy-free butter for Kerrygold or Plugrà butter.
But I would keep the dairy-free parmesan topping as is
because that stuff is good! It's a wonderful parmesan
cheese substitution for my dairy-free people. I got you!

Heat the olive oil and butter in a large, flat-bottomed
sauté pan over medium-high heat until the butter
bubbles. Add the garlic and cook for 1 minute, until
fragrant. Add the shrimp and cook for 2–3 minutes.
Stir in the green onion and dairy-free parm. Toss in the
hearts of palm pasta and cook for 4–5 minutes. Turn off
the heat and add the cherry tomatoes and lemon juice.
Serve garnished with additional dairy-free parm.

2 tablespoons olive oil

2 tablespoons dairy-free or
regular salted butter

1 teaspoon minced garlic

1 pound large shrimp, peeled and
deveined

2 tablespoons chopped green
onion

1 teaspoon Dairy-Free Parm
(recipe follows), plus more for
garnish

12 ounces hearts of palm linguine
(such as Palmini), rinsed and
drained

1 cup quartered cherry tomatoes

1 teaspoon lemon juice

DAIRY-FREE PARM

 YIELDS ¾ CUP

½ cup Brazil nuts

¼ cup nutritional yeast

½ teaspoon minced garlic

½ teaspoon salt

Combine all the ingredients in a mini food processor
or blender and pulse until it forms the crumbly consistency of grated parmesan. Use right away, or store in an
airtight container in the fridge for up to 7 days.

ULTIMATE LOW-CARB PIZZA

 YIELDS 1 (10–12-INCH) THIN-CRUST PIZZA

Olive oil spray

1½ cups shredded mozzarella cheese (if freshly shredded, pat dry after shredding)

3 tablespoons cream cheese, at room temperature

1 large egg

⅔ cup almond flour

½ teaspoon dried oregano

½ teaspoon dried basil

½ teaspoon garlic powder

Eat Happy Kitchen Tomato Basil Marinara or Home-made Tomato Basil Marinara (page 30)

Toppings of your choice (shredded mozzarella cheese, sliced veggies, meats, etc.)

THIS RECIPE AND THE TWO THAT FOLLOW WILL COVER *your pizza craving—hear me now, believe me after you make one! I started with this almond flour pizza crust in my first book, and I've made it so many times over the years, it's in my bones. I've also adapted this low-carb pizza crust in a lot of other applications, changing the spice and seasoning profile to suit any low-carb version of a flatbread.*

Preheat the oven to 425 degrees F. Line a rimmed baking sheet with parchment paper, then spray it lightly with olive oil spray.

In a large bowl, combine the mozzarella, cream cheese, egg, almond flour, oregano, basil, and garlic powder and mix well. Form the mixture into a ball.

Place the dough ball in the center of the prepared baking sheet and press it into a circle or square 10–12 inches wide and ¼ inch thick. Pierce the surface with a fork several times to prevent the crust from rising while baking. Bake for 6–8 minutes, until starting to turn golden, then flip the crust and bake for another 5–6 minutes, until the crust is starting to brown. Do not overbake as the crust may dry out.

Add the marinara and toppings and put the pizza back in the oven for 4–5 more minutes, until the top-ping cheese is melted and bubbly. Let cool slightly, then serve.

CAULIFLOWER PIZZA

 YIELDS 1 (10-INCH) THIN-CRUST PIZZA

Olive oil spray

2 (12-ounce) bags cauliflower
  florets or 1 large cauliflower
  head

¼ cup freshly grated parmesan
  cheese

¼ cup shredded mozzarella
  cheese (if freshly shredded,
  pat dry after shredding)

½ teaspoon dried oregano

½ teaspoon dried basil

½ teaspoon garlic powder

½ teaspoon salt

1 large egg

Eat Happy Kitchen Tomato
  Basil Marinara or Home-
  made Tomato Basil Marinara
  (page 30)

Toppings of your choice
  (shredded mozzarella cheese,
  sliced veggies, meats, etc.)

SADLY, MOST STORE-BOUGHT CAULIFLOWER CRUSTS *claim to be keto or low-carb but have cornstarch, potato starch, rice flour, and all kinds of binders and fillers in them. Make your cauliflower crust from scratch, I say! You can make your own cauliflower rice or buy it pre-grated. Always look for the finest-grated cauliflower you can find. Just remember to squeeze out that excess water, as that can cause the crust to fall apart.*

Preheat the oven to 425 degrees F. Line a rimmed baking sheet with parchment paper, then spray it lightly with olive oil spray.

Pulse the cauliflower florets in a food processor until it resembles the texture of couscous. It will have a snowy appearance. Transfer the cauliflower rice to a microwave-safe bowl and microwave on high for 3 minutes. Let cool. Using a cheesecloth, squeeze all excess water out of the cauliflower. Then do one final squeeze, wrapping a clean kitchen towel around the cheesecloth to make sure all excess water has been removed. This step is crucial.

Put the cauliflower rice in a large bowl, add the parmesan, mozzarella, oregano, basil, garlic powder, salt, and egg and mix well. Form the mixture into a ball.

Place the dough ball in the center of the prepared baking sheet and press it into a circle or square about 10 inches wide and ¼–½ inch thick. Bake for 11–14 minutes, until golden-brown spots start to cover the surface of the crust.

Add the marinara and toppings and return the pizza to the oven for 4–5 more minutes, until the topping cheese is melted and bubbly. Let cool slightly, then serve.

PORK RIND PIZZA

 YIELDS 1 (10–12-INCH) PIZZA

PORK RINDS ARE EVEN LOWER CARB THAN THE *almond flour and cauliflower found in the previous two crust recipes, so my keto-carnivore people love to make this crust. I am not a big fan of pork rinds on their own, even though they're a fantastic source of crunch in a low-carb or carnivore-forward diet. But they cook up so well in this pizza crust that you will have no idea you have crushed-up pork rinds in your pizza!*

Preheat the oven to 400 degrees F. Line a rimmed baking sheet with parchment paper, then spray it lightly with olive oil spray.

In a large bowl, combine the mozzarella, cream cheese, egg, pork rinds, oregano, basil, and garlic powder and mix well. Form the mixture into a ball.

Place the dough ball in the center of the prepared baking sheet and press it gently into a circle or square 10–12 inches wide and ¼–½ inch thick. Bake for 8–10 minutes, until the crust is starting to turn golden, then carefully flip the crust and bake for another 6–8 minutes, until the crust is starting to turn brown.

Add the marinara and toppings and return the pizza to the oven for 4–5 more minutes, until the topping cheese is melted and bubbly. Let cool slightly, then serve.

Olive oil spray

1½ cups shredded mozzarella cheese (if freshly shredded, pat dry after shredding)

3 tablespoons cream cheese, at room temperature

1 large egg

1 cup crushed pork rinds (I like Pork Panko)

½ teaspoon dried oregano

½ teaspoon dried basil

½ teaspoon garlic powder

Eat Happy Kitchen Tomato Basil Marinara or Home-made Tomato Basil Marinara (page 30)

Toppings of your choice (shredded mozzarella cheese, sliced veggies, meats, etc.)

KNIFE-AND-FORK CALZONE

 SERVES 2

CRUST

Olive oil spray

1½ cups shredded mozzarella
cheese (if freshly shredded,
pat dry after shredding)

3 tablespoons cream cheese, at
room temperature

1 large egg

1 cup almond flour

½ teaspoon dried oregano

½ teaspoon dried basil

½ teaspoon garlic powder

FILLING AND SAUCE

2 tablespoons pepperoni, cut into
bite-size pieces

¼–½ cup shredded mozzarella
cheese

1 tablespoon diced onion

1 tablespoon diced bell pepper
(any color)

1 tablespoon diced black olives

4–5 fresh basil leaves, torn

Eat Happy Kitchen Tomato
Basil Marinara or Home-
made Tomato Basil Marinara
(page 30), for dipping

USING OUR ALMOND FLOUR PIZZA CRUST RECIPE,
*we will now assemble a low-carb calzone. While it proba-
bly won't hold up to eating with your hands, it can certainly
be conquered with a knife and fork. That's just as delicious! You can use any assortment of meats, cheeses, and
veggies you like.*

Preheat the oven to 400 degrees F. Spray two pieces
of parchment paper with olive oil spray and place
one piece on a rimmed baking sheet.

For the crust: In a large bowl, combine the mozzarella, cream cheese, egg, almond flour, oregano, basil,
and garlic powder and mix well. Form the mixture into
a ball.

Place the dough ball on the prepared baking sheet
and cover it with the second sheet of oiled parchment
paper. Press out the dough into an even ¼" thin circle,
about 10" in diameter. Carefully remove the top piece
of parchment paper.

To fill the calzone: Place your preferred assortment
of the meat, cheese, and veggie filling ingredients onto
one half of the dough circle. Using the parchment paper
to lift it, carefully fold the empty side of the dough over
the filling with the parchment paper still attached to
the dough. Once folded, gently peel back the parchment
paper from the top of the calzone. Press the edges of
the dough to seal the calzone. If there are cracks in the
calzone, you can pinch extra dough off from the edges
and seal them.

Bake for 20–25 minutes, or until the crust is golden
brown and the cheese in the filling is melted (the
cheese will start to ooze out of the crust). Let rest for 5
minutes, then serve with a side of marinara for dipping.

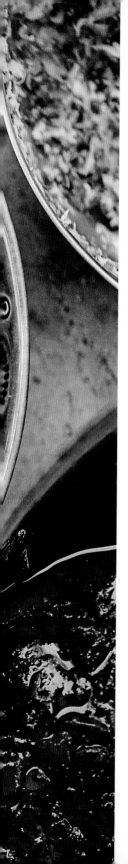

SECONDI PIATTI

Secondi piatti *means "second courses," and here's where our proteins can shine, as low carb is traditionally a meat-dominant way of eating. I've included Italian and Italian American classics made completely grain-free and gluten-free. There are some quick stove-top, easy-to-get-on-the-table main courses, and some Sunday slow-braise courses, but all are delicious and low carb.*

Osso Buco, page 108

PAN-SEARED BRANZINO

 SERVES 2

THIS RECIPE IS FOR A CLASSIC BRANZINO PREPARA-
tion without any flour coating because, frankly, you don't
need it. I like to leave the skin on the fillets because when
pan seared, it is crispy and delicious. Besides branzino,
this recipe works with most other white fishes, such as
halibut, cod, snapper, rockfish, sole, or tilapia.

1 pound branzino fillets, prefer-
ably skin-on

Salt and pepper

¼ teaspoon onion powder

¼ teaspoon garlic powder

2 tablespoons olive oil

¼ cup chopped kalamata olives

1 teaspoon grated lemon zest

Juice of ½ lemon (about 1 tablespoon)

2 tablespoons fresh oregano
leaves

1 tablespoon drained capers

Lemon wedges, for serving

Season the branzino fillets all over with salt and
pepper. Sprinkle the onion powder and garlic powder on the flesh side.

Heat the olive oil in a large nonstick sauté pan over
medium-high heat until shimmering. Add the branzino
and cook until cooked through, 2–3 minutes per side,
then transfer to serving plates.

Add the olives, lemon zest, lemon juice, oregano, and
capers to the pan. Cook for 2–3 minutes, then pour the
mixture over the branzino and serve garnished with
lemon wedges.

SALMON PUTTANESCA

 SERVES 4–5

2 tablespoons olive oil, divided

½ medium onion, diced

1 teaspoon minced garlic

¾ cup pitted black olives, chopped

2 tablespoons drained capers

½ teaspoon onion powder

½ teaspoon red pepper flakes

1 teaspoon salt, divided, plus more for seasoning

7–10 fresh basil leaves, chopped

1 teaspoon chopped fresh oregano leaves, plus more for garnish

2 (14-ounce) cans no-sugar-added diced tomatoes, 1 can pureed in a blender

6 tablespoons tomato paste

½ teaspoon black pepper, plus more for seasoning

1½ pounds skin-on salmon fillets

THE PUTTANESCA SAUCE IN THIS RECIPE TAKES THE *base of my marinara and adds hearty ingredients to make it almost into a stew. Of course, Eat Happy Kitchen has the best jarred puttanesca on store shelves, and it's all based on my recipe that I've been making for years (which is a perfect complement to roasted salmon). If you're using wild-caught salmon, reduce the cook time on the salmon to closer to 12–15 minutes, as it's thinner and cooks much more quickly.*

Preheat the oven to 350 degrees F.

Heat 1 tablespoon of the olive oil in a large saucepan over medium-high heat. Add the onion and garlic and cook until soft, 3–4 minutes. Add the olives, capers, onion powder, red pepper flakes, ½ teaspoon of the salt, basil, and oregano and cook, stirring occasionally, for 2–3 minutes, until fragrant. Stir in the tomatoes with their juices, tomato paste, remaining ½ teaspoon salt, and black pepper. Bring to a boil, then turn the heat down and simmer for 15–20 minutes. Season with additional salt and black pepper, if needed.

Meanwhile, season the salmon fillets well with salt and pepper. Drizzle a large baking pan with the remaining 1 tablespoon of the olive oil, then place the salmon fillets skin side down in the pan. Bake for 15–20 minutes, or to the desired doneness. (Alternatively, you can grill the salmon fillets skin side down for about 10 minutes, or to the desired doneness.)

To serve, ladle some sauce into shallow bowls, then place a salmon fillet on top. Garnish with fresh oregano.

SHRIMP FRA DIAVOLO

 SERVES 4

FRA DIAVOLO MEANS "THE BROTHER OF THE DEVIL."
This sauce is often confused with arrabbiata sauce as they
are both spicy, but traditionally, fra diavolo is made with-
out pancetta. It's perfect with shrimp or shellfish.

1 pint cherry tomatoes, halved
(about 2 cups)

4 tablespoons olive oil, divided

Salt and black pepper

1 medium onion, chopped

1 garlic clove, minced

1 teaspoon red pepper flakes or
Calabrian pepper flakes

1 tablespoon white wine vinegar

2 pounds large shrimp, peeled
and deveined

2 tablespoons chopped fresh flat-
leaf parsley, for garnish

Preheat the oven to 350 degrees F.
Toss the cherry tomato halves on a rimmed baking
sheet with 2 tablespoons of the olive oil. Season well
with salt and black pepper. Roast for 20–25 minutes,
until the tomatoes are soft and starting to blister. Remove from the oven and set aside.

In a large, flat-bottomed nonstick sauté pan, heat
the remaining 2 tablespoons olive oil over medium
heat. Add the onion and cook until soft, 3–4 minutes.
Add the garlic and cook for 1–2 minutes, until fragrant.
Stir in the pepper flakes and vinegar and season with
salt and black pepper. Add the shrimp and cook for 2–3
minutes, until the shrimp are cooked through. Add the
roasted tomatoes and any juices that have collected on
the baking sheet and toss with the shrimp until hot.
Season once more with salt and black pepper if needed.
Serve immediately, garnished with the parsley.

SCALLOPS WITH AGRODOLCE SAUCE

 SERVES 3 AS AN APPETIZER OR 2 AS A MAIN COURSE

⅓ cup dried cherries, chopped

¼ cup sherry vinegar

⅓ cup plus 2 tablespoons olive oil, divided

¼ cup raw almonds, chopped

2 shallots, thinly sliced into rings

½ teaspoon Calabrian pepper flakes

Salt and black pepper

1–2 pounds sea scallops, patted dry

Chopped fresh flat-leaf parsley, for garnish

THE SILKY RICHNESS OF SCALLOPS GOES PERFECTLY *with this pungent sauce. Note that the agrodolce sauce needs to be made at least 8 hours ahead of time, but you can do that in the morning or the night before and have dinner on the table in about 7 minutes from start to finish. Pro tip: Most sea scallops are pumped full of water before they're frozen and transported, so make sure you let them thaw completely and pat them dry as much as possible. Even then, they will release excess water when you cook them, so be careful not to overcook.*

In a small bowl, soak the dried cherries in the sherry vinegar and set aside.

Heat ⅓ cup of olive oil in a large sauté pan over medium heat. Add the almonds and toast until they just start to turn golden brown and become fragrant, 2–3 minutes. Remove the pan from the heat and let cool.

Add the shallots and Calabrian pepper flakes to the bowl with the soaking cherries. Add the cooled nuts and oil. Stir in 1 teaspoon salt. Cover the bowl and refrigerate for at least 8 hours.

Remove the agrodolce sauce from the fridge and bring it to room temperature.

Season the scallops well with salt and pepper. In a large cast-iron skillet, heat the remaining 2 tablespoons of olive oil over medium-high heat. Starting at the 12 o'clock position, place the scallops in a circle in the pan and sear for 1–2 minutes, then flip the scallops, again starting at the 12 o'clock position, and sear for another 1–2 minutes, until cooked through. Transfer the scallops to serving plates, top with a generous portion of agrodolce sauce, and garnish with parsley. Serve immediately.

CHICKEN PICCATA

 SERVES 2–3

MUCH LIKE THE BELOVED CHICKEN PARMESAN
*(page 89), chicken piccata is a classic Italian restaurant
menu item. It's next to impossible to find grain-free or
even gluten-free versions of this delicious dish out in the
world. So let's make it at home with fresh ingredients, and
you'll never be tempted to order the high-carb version
again.*

Season the chicken cutlets well with salt and pepper.
In a shallow dish, whisk together the almond flour,
garlic powder, and onion powder. Dredge the chicken
cutlets in the flour mixture.

Heat 2 tablespoons of the olive oil in a large,
flat-bottomed sauté pan over medium-high heat until
shimmering. Working in batches, cook the chicken
cutlets until cooked through, 3–4 minutes per side,
adding more olive oil to the pan as needed. Transfer the
chicken breasts to a plate.

Add the broth and vinegar to the pan and bring to
a boil. Cook for 1–2 minutes, then add the lemon juice
and capers. Turn the heat down to medium and let the
sauce cook 5–7 minutes or until thickened. Add the
butter and cook until it's melted, then whisk the sauce.
Season with salt and pepper to taste.

Return the chicken cutlets to the pan and spoon the
sauce over them. Transfer the cutlets to serving plates,
pour the remaining sauce over them, and garnish with
the parsley.

1–1½ pounds boneless, skinless
chicken breasts, butterflied
and pounded ¼ inch thick

Salt and pepper

1 cup almond flour or crushed
pork rinds (such as Pork
Panko)

½ teaspoon garlic powder

½ teaspoon onion powder

3–4 tablespoons olive oil, divided

¾ cup chicken broth

¼ cup white wine vinegar *or* ⅓
cup dry white wine

Juice of 1 lemon (about 2 tablespoons)

¼ cup drained capers

2 tablespoons salted butter

¼ cup chopped fresh flat-leaf
parsley, for garnish

PAN-FRIED CHICKEN THIGHS WITH SAGE

 SERVES 2–4

1–2 pounds boneless, skinless chicken thighs, cut into 1-inch pieces

Salt and pepper

2 tablespoons olive oil

2 tablespoons salted butter

1 shallot, finely chopped

¼ cup white wine vinegar or white balsamic vinegar

3 tablespoons chopped fresh sage leaves

THIS IS AN EASY WEEKNIGHT VERSION OF WHAT'S *known as vinegar chicken, but instead of bone-in, skin-on thighs, we use boneless to save time on prep and cooking without sacrificing any flavor.*

Season the chicken pieces well with salt and pepper. Heat the olive oil and butter in a large sauté pan over medium-high heat. Add the shallot and cook for 1–2 minutes, until soft. Add the chicken pieces and cook, tossing occasionally, for 5–6 minutes, until cooked through. Transfer the chicken to a plate.

Add the vinegar to the pan and scrape up any browned bits from the bottom. Add the sage and cook for 1 minute. Return the chicken pieces to the pan, along with any juices that have collected on the plate, and toss them in the sage vinegar. Season with salt and pepper. Turn the heat to low, cover, and simmer for 4–5 minutes. Serve.

CHICKEN PARMESAN

 SERVES 2–4

THIS CROWD-PLEASING DISH, WHICH FIRST APPEARED *in my OG cookbook* Eat Happy, *is such a beloved Italian American classic that I had to include it here—this time with options for my dairy-free people.*

Preheat the oven to 350 degrees F.

Season the chicken breasts well with salt and pepper. In a shallow bowl, whisk together the almond flour, garlic powder, onion powder, oregano, and basil. Dredge the chicken breasts in the almond flour mixture to coat.

Heat the olive oil in a large sauté pan over medium-high heat. Working in batches, add the chicken and cook for 6–7 minutes per side, until cooked through. Add more oil between batches as needed. Transfer to a large baking pan in a single layer.

Sprinkle half of the mozzarella on the chicken. Ladle the marinara over the chicken, covering it but reserving some for serving. Sprinkle the remaining mozzarella and the parmesan over the marinara. Bake for 10 minutes, or until the cheese is melted and bubbly.

Meanwhile, warm the reserved marinara in a small saucepan over medium-low heat. Serve the chicken with the sauce.

1–2 pounds boneless, skinless chicken breasts, trimmed and pounded ½ inch thick

Salt and pepper

1 cup almond flour or crushed pork rinds (such as Pork Panko)

½ teaspoon garlic powder

½ teaspoon onion powder

½ teaspoon dried oregano

½ teaspoon dried basil

2 tablespoons olive oil, plus more if needed

1 cup shredded mozzarella cheese or dairy-free mozzarella cheese (I like Violife and Parmela brands)

1 (26-ounce) jar Eat Happy Kitchen Tomato Basil Marinara *or* 3 cups Homemade Tomato Basil Marinara (page 30)

½ cup freshly grated parmesan cheese or Dairy-Free Parm (page 65)

CHICKEN SALTIMBOCCA

 SERVES 3–4

2 pounds boneless, skinless chicken breasts, pounded ¼ inch thick

Salt and pepper

4–6 slices prosciutto

7–10 fresh sage leaves

2 tablespoons olive oil, plus more for pan frying, if necessary

¼ cup chicken broth

3 tablespoons white wine vinegar

4 tablespoons (½ stick) cold salted butter, cubed

SALTIMBOCCA IS TRADITIONALLY MADE WITH VEAL *cutlets, but you can also use thin boneless pork chops or a pounded-out beef steak. My version uses two of my favorite proteins, chicken and prosciutto, combined into one flavor that jumps in your mouth (the translation of saltimbocca).*

Season the chicken cutlets with salt and pepper. Lay a slice of prosciutto on top of each chicken piece, then cover it with 1–2 sage leaves and secure with a toothpick.

Heat the olive oil in a large, flat-bottomed sauté pan over medium-high heat. Working in batches, add the chicken cutlets, prosciutto side up, and cook for 4–5 minutes, then gently flip the chicken and cook until the chicken is cooked through and the prosciutto is crispy, another 3–5 minutes. Add more olive oil between batches as needed. Transfer the chicken to a paper towel–lined plate.

Remove the pan from the burner for about 1 minute, then place it back on the heat and pour in the broth. The broth will bubble up. Scrape up any browned bits in the pan. Stir in the vinegar, bring to a boil, and cook for 1–2 minutes. Add the cold butter cubes and whisk them into the sauce for 3–4 minutes, until a smooth, creamy sauce forms.

Turn off the heat, return the chicken to the pan, and spoon the sauce over them. Carefully remove the toothpicks and serve immediately.

STEVE'S SPIEDINI

 SERVES 4

1 tablespoon olive oil, plus more for drizzling

1 white onion, half minced, half set aside

2 celery stalks, chopped

2 carrots, chopped

Salt and pepper

1 teaspoon minced garlic

½ teaspoon dried oregano

½ teaspoon dried basil

1¼ cups almond flour, divided

¼ cup tomato paste

1 cup freshly grated parmesan cheese

2–3 pounds boneless, skinless chicken breasts, butterflied and pounded ¼ inch thick

12 fresh bay leaves (optional)

4 large eggs, beaten

Eat Happy Kitchen Tomato Basil Marinara or Homemade Tomato Basil Marinara (page 30), for dipping (optional)

MY FRIEND STEVE PASSANTINO INTRODUCED ME TO *spiedini, which are basically Italian meat kabobs. Sicilian, to be more precise—which makes sense since Steve's Sicilian nonna used to make these for him. He passed along the recipe to me and, of course, I put the low-carb spin on it so we can all enjoy Italian kebabs and pretend Steve's darling nonna made them for us. These can be made with chicken, lamb, beef, or pork cutlets. If you're using wooden skewers, make sure you soak them in water for 10 minutes before using.*

Preheat the oven to 400 degrees F.

In a large, flat-bottomed sauté pan, heat the olive oil over medium-high heat. Add the minced onion, celery, and carrots and cook until very soft, 4–5 minutes. Season well with salt and pepper. Add the garlic and cook for 1–2 minutes, until fragrant. Stir in the oregano and basil and cook for 1–2 more minutes. Stir in ¼ cup of the almond flour, then the tomato paste and parmesan, and cook until heated and well mixed, 3–4 minutes. Remove the pan from the heat and set aside.

Season the chicken well with salt and pepper. Spoon a tablespoon or two of the veggie mixture onto the center of a chicken piece. Roll the chicken snugly around the stuffing. Repeat with the remaining chicken pieces and veggie mixture.

Cut the remaining half onion in half again and separate those halves into pieces.

On each skewer, thread a rolled-up spiedino, a piece of onion, and a bay leaf if desired, then repeat until the skewer is full (but not over full). You should have four skewers.

Line up three rimmed baking sheets. On one baking sheet, pour the beaten eggs. On the next baking sheet, pour the remaining 1 cup almond flour. Dredge each skewer in the eggs, roll them in the almond flour, then lay the skewer on the third (clean) baking sheet. Drizzle the skewers liberally with olive oil and season once more with salt.

Bake for 25–30 minutes, until the chicken is cooked through and the coating is starting to turn golden brown. Serve with marinara for dipping or drizzled with more olive oil.

ROASTED LEMON TUSCAN CHICKEN

 SERVES 4–6

THIS IS A CLASSIC ROASTED TUSCAN CHICKEN DISH. *If you have charcoal or a pellet smoker to roast it in, all the better. But an oven makes this roasted chicken more than sufficiently delicious.*

5–6 pounds bone-in, skin-on chicken pieces

Salt and pepper

4 tablespoons salted butter, at room temperature

1 teaspoon chopped fresh rosemary leaves

½ teaspoon thyme leaves

1 teaspoon minced garlic

2 lemons, cut into wedges

Olive oil, for drizzling

Preheat the oven to 425 degrees F. Line a large rimmed baking sheet with parchment paper.

Place the chicken in a single layer on the prepared baking sheet. Season well with salt and pepper.

In a small bowl, combine the butter, rosemary, thyme, and garlic to make a compound butter. Smear the compound butter all over the chicken pieces. Place the lemon wedges between the chicken pieces. Drizzle olive oil over the chicken.

Bake for 15 minutes, then turn the oven temperature down to 350 degrees F and bake for 20–25 minutes more, until the chicken is cooked through (an instant-read thermometer inserted into a thigh should read 165 degrees F).

Squeeze the cooked lemon wedges over the chicken and serve.

MEATBALLS AND SAUCE

 YIELDS 18–20 (2-INCH) MEATBALLS

1 pound high-fat ground beef

1 pound high-fat ground veal or pork

½ cup almond flour or crushed pork rinds (such as Pork Panko)

2–3 slices Genoa or dry salami, minced

3 large eggs

1 tablespoon yellow mustard

1 teaspoon minced garlic

1 teaspoon minced fresh parsley

2 teaspoons salt

½ teaspoon pepper

½ teaspoon garlic powder

½ teaspoon onion powder

½ teaspoon dried oregano

½ teaspoon dried basil

2 (26-ounce) jars Eat Happy Kitchen Tomato Basil Marinara, Puttanesca Sauce, or Arrabbiata Spicy Marinara (or make your own—see pages 30–32)

MEATBALLS AND SAUCE ARE THE GO-TO FOR SUNDAY *dinner in Italian American homes. I like to serve these meatballs—which are based on my husband's grand-mother's recipe—with roasted spaghetti squash pasta (see page 58) or sautéed zucchini noodles, or I just eat them with sauce until my belly is full. You can choose any red sauce for this recipe.*

Preheat the oven to 400 degrees F.

In a large bowl, combine all the ingredients except the sauce and mix well with your hands. Roll the mixture into 2-inch balls and place them close together on a rimmed baking sheet. Bake for 20 minutes, or until cooked through. Transfer the meatballs to a large saucepan, add the sauce, and bring to a boil over medium-high heat. Reduce the heat and simmer, covered, for at least 30 minutes or up to 2 hours. Serve.

STEAK MARSALA

 SERVES 4-6

MAKE STEAK MARSALA AS A SPECIAL TREAT, AS THIS *recipe uses filet mignon as the star of the dish. Marsala sauce uses Marsala wine, herbs, mushrooms, broth, and butter to make it come to life. Marsala wine has a fairly sweet flavor profile, though, so we're going to lessen the impact of the sugar in this dish by switching out the wine for sherry vinegar, which is available at most grocery stores and online. Just check the label for no sugar added.*

2 pounds filet mignon, cut into 1-inch pieces

Salt and pepper

1 tablespoon olive oil

½ sweet onion, chopped

2 garlic cloves, minced

1 pound baby portobello or cremini mushrooms, thinly sliced

1 cup beef broth

¼ cup sherry vinegar

1 teaspoon fresh thyme leaves

1 tablespoon salted butter

2 tablespoons heavy cream

1 teaspoon chopped fresh flat-leaf parsley, for garnish

Season the steak well with salt and pepper. Heat the olive oil in a large cast-iron skillet or flat-bottomed sauté pan over medium-high heat until shimmering. Add the steak pieces and sear for 1–2 minutes, turning to brown on all sides. Transfer the steak to a plate, reserving the juices in the pan.

Add the onion to the pan and cook for 2–3 minutes, until softened. Add the garlic and cook for 1–2 minutes, until fragrant. Add the mushrooms and toss to coat them with the onion, garlic, and pan juices. Season with salt and pepper. When the mushrooms start to brown on the outside, pour in the broth and vinegar. Bring the mixture to a boil, then lower the heat to a simmer, add the thyme, and season with salt and pepper. Simmer for 5–7 minutes, until slightly reduced and thickened. Whisk in the butter and cream and cook for 2–3 more minutes, until heated through. Season the sauce once more with salt and pepper, if needed. Turn off the heat, return the steak to the pan, and stir to coat. Serve the steak topped with the sauce and garnished with the parsley.

BISTECCA ALLA FIORENTINA

 SERVES 2

1 large (14–16 ounce) porterhouse, T-bone, or bone-in rib eye steak

Salt and pepper

1 teaspoon minced garlic

Juice of ½ lemon (about 1 table-spoon)

1 teaspoon minced fresh rose-mary leaves

THIS PHOTO SHOWS STEAK COOKED TWO WAYS: ON A *grill (top) and in a pan (bottom). Both are delicious, so find the largest bone-in fatty piece of steak you can, and get to cooking it the traditional Tuscan way—with lots of salt and heat.*

Heat a grill to 500 degrees F, or heat a large cast-iron skillet over high heat.

Season the steak liberally with salt and pepper. Grill or pan-sear the steak for 4–7 minutes per side for medium-rare. After flipping the steak, reduce the heat to 400 degrees F on the grill or to medium on the stove. Do not press the steak with a spatula while cooking as this will squeeze out the precious juices!

While the steak is cooking, in a small bowl, whisk together the garlic, lemon juice, rosemary, and salt and pepper to taste. Remove the steak from the heat and rub it using a spoon, pastry brush, or basting mop with the garlic-lemon-rosemary mixture while it rests for 5 minutes. Slice and serve.

BRACIOLA (Stuffed Flank Steak)

 SERVES 4–6

2 tablespoons raw pine nuts

1 (2–3-pound) flank steak or skirt
    steak

Salt and pepper

1 tablespoon olive oil

½ onion, diced

1 yellow, orange, or red bell
    pepper, cored and diced

1 teaspoon minced garlic

3 cups baby spinach

¼ cup freshly grated parmesan
    cheese

4 slices prosciutto, loosely
    chopped

1 (26-ounce) jar Eat Happy
    Kitchen Tomato Basil Mar-
    inara *or* 3 cups Homemade
    Tomato Basil Marinara
    (page 30)

2 rosemary sprigs

HERE'S ANOTHER ROLLED-UP DISH, ALONG WITH
*Steve's Spiedini (page 92) and Eggplant Involtini (page 164).
I don't know why we love rolling up our food, but we do!
I love making braciola for Sunday dinner every once in
awhile to change it up from meatballs and sauce. It's a
great use of flank steak, which I feel is an underappreci-
ated cut of meat.*

Preheat the oven to 400 degrees F.

In a small sauté pan, toast the pine nuts over
medium-high heat until they start to turn brown and
are fragrant. Transfer them to a bowl.

Season the steak liberally with salt and pepper.
Cover the steak with a large piece of parchment paper
and pound it with the textured side of a meat tenderizer to ½ inch thick. Discard the parchment and set the
steak aside on a rimmed baking sheet.

In a large, flat-bottomed sauté pan, heat the olive oil
over medium-high heat. Add the onion and cook until
soft, 2–3 minutes. Add the bell pepper and cook for 2–3
minutes, until soft. Add the garlic and cook, stirring, for
1–2 minutes, until fragrant. Add the spinach and toss
until wilted, about 2 minutes. Season with salt and pepper. Remove the pan from the heat and add the parmesan and toasted pine nuts. Let cool for 5 minutes.

Spread the veggie mixture evenly over the steak,
then scatter the chopped prosciutto pieces evenly atop
the veggie mixture. From the widest side of the flank
steak, carefully roll the steak into a log. Tie the log up
tightly with kitchen string every few inches, making
sure to keep the stuffing from falling out. You may
need a second set of hands to help with this step.

Reheat the sauté pan over medium-high heat and brown the flank steak log on all sides, about 2 minutes per side.

Place the rolled, stuffed steak log in the center of a large roasting pan. Pour the marinara over and around the flank steak. Drop in the rosemary sprigs, cover with aluminum foil, and bake for 60–90 minutes, or until the steak is tender when pierced with a fork.

Remove the foil, then carefully cut away and discard the kitchen string. Remove and discard the rosemary sprigs. Slice the steak log into 1½-inch slices, top with the sauce from the pan, and serve.

Pictured on pages 104–105

Braciola (Stuffed Flank Steak), recipe page 102

NORTHERN ITALIAN BEEF ROAST

 SERVES 4–6

I'M A HUGE FAN OF POT ROAST. IT'S THE ULTIMATE *comfort food. Every culture seems to have their version of a slow-cooked, inexpensive cut of meat, and the Italians are no different. This pot roast is influenced by Northern Italian cuisine, where the German-Austrian influence of cooking meats with milk is prevalent.*

1 (2–3-pound) chuck roast, top round, or bottom round roast

Salt and pepper

4 tablespoons salted butter

1 large carrot, chopped

2 celery stalks, chopped

⅓ cup white wine vinegar

1 cup whole milk

1 cup beef or chicken broth

2–3 rosemary sprigs

Season the roast liberally with salt and pepper. In a Dutch oven or other large pot, heat the butter over medium-high heat until it's bubbling. Add the carrot and celery and cook until soft, 3–4 minutes. Add the roast and brown it on all sides, 1–2 minutes per side. Transfer the roast to a plate.

Pour the vinegar into the pot and cook for 1–2 minutes, scraping up any bits stuck to the bottom of the pot. The vinegar should boil and then start to evaporate. Return the roast to the pot and pour the milk and broth over it. Toss in the rosemary sprigs and season with salt and pepper. Bring to a boil, then cover, reduce the heat, and simmer for 2½–3 hours. The roast should be fork-tender. If it isn't, cook for another 30 minutes, then check again. When ready, transfer the roast to a cutting board and let stand for 10 minutes. Slice and serve, topping it with the vegetables and juices from the pot.

OSSO BUCO

 SERVES 4–5

3–4 pounds veal, beef, or lamb shanks, horizontally cut into 4–5 portions

Salt and pepper

2 tablespoons olive oil

¼ cup chopped pancetta

½ onion, chopped

2 carrots, chopped

2 celery stalks, chopped

¼ cup white wine vinegar

½ cup beef broth

1 (14-ounce) can no-sugar-added diced tomatoes

Bouquet garni (a bundle of fresh rosemary sprigs, bay leaves, thyme sprigs, oregano sprigs, and/or sage leaves tied with kitchen string)

3 tablespoons minced fresh flat-leaf parsley

1 tablespoon grated lemon zest

1 teaspoon minced garlic

Cauliflower Mash Polenta (page 152), for serving

USUALLY OSSO BUCO IS AN ITALIAN RESTAURANT *specialty, but with a little prep and planning, you can make this version at home. Serve with the easy-to-make Cauliflower Mash Polenta (page 152) for the full experience. Have your butcher cut the shanks horizontally (called crosscut) so the bone marrow is exposed and can simmer out in the cooking process, tenderizing the rougher shank cut to be fork-tender. If your butcher trusses up each portion for you, don't forget to cut and remove the kitchen string before serving.*

Season the shanks well with salt and pepper. In a Dutch oven or other large pot, heat the olive oil over medium-high heat. Add the pancetta and cook for 4–5 minutes, until the pancetta is softened and starting to crisp. Using a slotted spoon, transfer the pancetta to a paper towel–lined plate. Add the shanks to the pot and brown all sides, 2–3 minutes per side. Transfer the shanks to a plate.

Add the onion, carrots, and celery to the pot and cook until they start to soften, 4–5 minutes. Season with salt and pepper. Add the vinegar, broth, tomatoes with their juices, and bouquet garni and bring to a boil. Season with salt and pepper. Return the pancetta and shanks to the pot and spoon the liquid over the shanks. Season again with salt and pepper, lower the heat to medium-low, cover, and cook until the shanks are fork-tender, 2½–3 hours.

In a small bowl, combine the parsley, lemon zest, and garlic to make a garnish called gremolata.

To serve, scoop the cauliflower mash polenta into shallow bowls, then place a shank on top with a ladle of pan juices and top with a spoonful of the gremolata.

VEAL MILANESE

 SERVES 2

VEAL CUTLETS ARE AN ITALIAN RESTAURANT STAPLE, *and the cooking technique is the same used for the chicken cutlets in Chicken Piccata (page 85) and Chicken Parmesan (page 89). If you can't find veal at your local market, you can use pounded boneless chicken breasts or pork chops.*

1 pound veal cutlets, pounded thin

Salt and pepper

2 large eggs

2 tablespoons heavy cream

1 cup almond flour

3 tablespoons salted butter

Lemon wedges, for garnish

Fresh parsley, for garnish

Season the veal cutlets with salt and pepper. In a shallow bowl, whisk together the eggs and cream. Put the almond flour in a second shallow bowl.

Heat the butter in a large cast-iron skillet or nonstick sauté pan over medium-high heat until bubbling. Dredge one cutlet in the egg wash, then coat with the almond flour and place it in the hot pan. Repeat with as many of the remaining cutlets as will fit in the pan. If you run out of room, cook the cutlets in batches.

Fry the cutlets for 4–5 minutes per side, until cooked through. Transfer to plates, garnish with lemon wedges and fresh parsley, and serve.

STUFFED PORK CHOPS

 SERVES 4

2 tablespoons olive oil

4 boneless pork chops, at least 1 inch thick

Salt and pepper

½ cup freshly grated parmesan cheese

1 tablespoon tomato paste

1 tablespoon balsamic vinegar

1 teaspoon finely minced fresh rosemary leaves

⅓ cup pine nuts

1 plum, pitted and finely chopped

STUFFED PORK CHOPS MAKE PORK CHOPS A LITTLE *more interesting. Just watch the cook time so you don't dry them out. If you'd like to use bone-in pork chops, have at it. Just increase your cook time to about 45 minutes so the meat close to the bone cooks through.*

Preheat the oven to 400 degrees F. Drizzle a large baking dish with the olive oil.

To butterfly the pork chops, slice them in half horizontally almost all the way, so the two halves are still attached and can open up like a book. Using a meat tenderizer, pound the pork chops until they're ½ inch thick. Season well on both sides with salt and pepper. Place the pork chops in a single layer in the prepared baking dish.

In a medium bowl, combine the parmesan, tomato paste, vinegar, and rosemary to form a paste. Fold in the pine nuts and plum pieces. Spoon one-quarter of the stuffing onto half of each pork chop. Close each pork chop over the stuffing and hold them together with a few toothpicks.

Bake for 20–25 minutes, until just cooked through (you may need to cut one open to check the doneness); do not overcook the chops. Remove from the oven and let stand for 5 minutes, then remove and discard the toothpicks. Serve pork chops with the pan juices spooned over.

ROASTED BONE-IN PORK CHOPS

 SERVES 2–3

ONE-PAN DISHES ARE THE ULTIMATE EASY WEEK-
*night meal. This recipe combines delish pork chops with
some root veggies and pearl onions for the perfect cool-
weather comfort food.*

P reheat the oven to 425 degrees F.
Season the pork chops well with salt and pepper.
In a baking dish or large, shallow bowl, mix the olive oil,
oregano, basil, and garlic. Dredge the pork chops in the
mixture to coat.

Put the parsnips, carrots, and pearl onions on a
rimmed baking sheet, season with salt and pepper,
and drizzle with olive oil. Bake for 15 minutes. Remove
the sheet from the oven, stir the veggies, and add the
broccolini and pork chops to the sheet. Season the
broccolini with salt and pepper and a drizzle of olive
oil. Reduce the oven temperature to 350 degrees F and
bake for 15 minutes, or until the pork chops are cooked
through.

Serve the chops alongside the roasted veggies. If
you'd like more color on your pork chops, you can sear
them in the pan for 2 minutes per side after baking
them.

1–2 pounds bone-in pork chops

Salt and pepper

2 tablespoons olive oil, plus more
for drizzling

1 teaspoon dried oregano

1 teaspoon dried basil

1 teaspoon minced garlic

2–3 parsnips, peeled and halved
lengthwise if thick

2–3 carrots, peeled and halved
lengthwise if thick

1 cup pearl onions

1 bunch broccolini

BRAISED PORK MEDALLIONS

 SERVES 3–4

2–3 pounds pork tenderloins

Salt and pepper

3 tablespoons olive oil

2 garlic cloves, minced

1 pint baby portobello or cremini
mushrooms, chopped

2 tablespoons balsamic vinegar

7–10 fresh basil leaves, chopped

1 teaspoon chopped fresh rosemary leaves

¼ cup chopped roasted red
peppers

PORK TENDERLOIN IS AN AFFORDABLE CUT OF MEAT
*that's very flavorful. Slicing the tenderloin into medallions
makes this dish a no-brainer to get dinner on the table
quickly while maintaining a tender, melt-in-your-mouth,
high-quality dish.*

———————————————————

Slice the pork tenderloins into 1-inch-thick pieces.
Pound them thin and season well with salt and
pepper.

Heat the olive oil in a large, flat-bottomed sauté pan
over medium-high heat. Add the garlic and cook for
1 minute, until fragrant. Add the mushrooms and cook
for 3–4 minutes, until seared and starting to soften.
Season with salt and pepper. Stir in the vinegar, basil,
rosemary, and roasted red peppers. Working in batches
if necessary, add the pork medallions and sear them
on each side, about 1 minute per side Cover, reduce the
heat to medium-low, and cook for 4–5 minutes, until
cooked through. The pork should be a touch pink on the
inside and still tender. Season once more with salt and
pepper. Serve with the veggies and pan sauce.

PORCHETTA

 SERVES 6–8

1 (3–4-pound) pork loin, shoulder, or butt, butterflied

1 pork belly large enough to cover the pork loin when it's rolled up

Salt and black pepper

⅓–½ cup olive oil, plus more for drizzling

3 garlic cloves

1 tablespoon fresh thyme leaves

1 tablespoon fresh oregano leaves

1 tablespoon fresh rosemary leaves

1 tablespoon fresh flat-leaf parsley leaves

1 teaspoon ground coriander

1 teaspoon fennel seeds

1 teaspoon finely minced orange or lemon zest

½ teaspoon red pepper flakes

½ cup water

THIS RECIPE IS A SHOWSTOPPER AND REALLY PRETTY *easy to make. You just need to ask your butcher to butter-fly the pork loin for you. And if you can, prep the roast a day before cooking it to dry out the outward-facing fatty skin of the pork belly so it will get crispy while roasting. If you have a smoker, you are welcome to smoke the porchetta as it cooks, but oven roasting works amazingly well.*

Season the butterflied pork loin and pork belly well on both sides with salt and black pepper. Score the pork loin with a crosshatch pattern on the side facing up. Score the pork belly with a crosshatch pattern on the fatty skin side.

In a mini food processor or blender, combine ⅓ cup olive oil, the garlic, thyme, oregano, rosemary, parsley, coriander, fennel, zest, pepper flakes, and 1 teaspoon salt and blend into a smooth, green herb paste, adding more oil as needed to achieve the desired consistency. Spread the herb paste evenly all over the face-up side of the pork loin. Roll up the pork loin tightly. Season the outside of the rolled-up pork loin once more with salt. Wrap the rolled-up pork loin with the pork belly, fatty skin side out. Truss well with kitchen string to hold it all together into one large cylindrical roast. Place the porchetta on a wire rack in a roasting pan and refrigerate, uncovered, overnight.

Preheat the oven to 250 degrees F.

Remove the roast from the fridge and let stand at room temperature for 30 minutes while the oven preheats. Pour the water into the bottom of the pan. Roast on the lowest oven rack for 3–5 hours, or until the center of the roast reads 145 degrees F on an instant-read

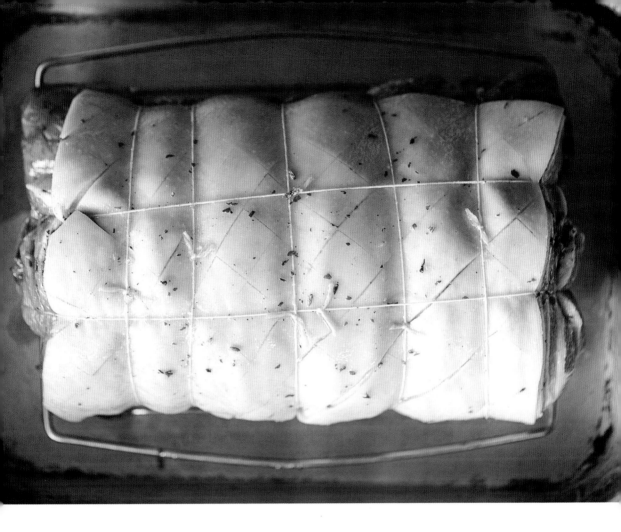

thermometer. If the outer skin doesn't crisp up, you can turn the oven up to 500 degrees F and crisp the skin for 5–7 minutes at the very end of the roasting process.

Remove the roast from the oven and let stand for 15–20 minutes. Carefully cut and discard the kitchen string. Slice the porchetta roast into 1-inch-thick slices and serve with juices from the pan.

Finished Porchetta pictured on pages 120–121

Porchetta, recipe page 118

SOUPS, STEWS, AND CASSEROLES

I'm gonna cop to the fact that you won't find a "Soups, Stews, and Casseroles" section on most Italian restaurant menus. This chapter is my own collection of hearty dishes that are absolutely scrumptious but rarely found gluten- or grain-free out in the wild. In my brain, these dishes deserve their own chapter. Take matters into your own hands and make a low-carb lasagna or manicotti. You'll be so glad you did. And like the Primi Piatti chapter, you won't miss the pasta.

Stuffed Manicotti, page 141

CIOPPINO (Jeannie's Seafood Stew)

 SERVES 8

⅓ cup olive oil

1 fennel bulb, rough ends and top discarded, chopped

2 celery stalks, finely chopped

1 sweet onion, minced

2 teaspoons minced garlic

1 tablespoon dried oregano

⅛ teaspoon red pepper flakes

Salt and black pepper

1 pound squid tubes, cut into ½-inch pieces

1 cup chicken broth

1 cup clam juice

1 tablespoon grated lemon zest

Juice of ½ lemon (about 1 tablespoon)

2 (14-ounce) cans no-sugar-added diced tomatoes, 1 can pureed in a blender

2 tablespoons tomato paste

1 pound large shrimp, peeled and deveined

1 pound cod, halibut, haddock, or other white fish, cut into 2-inch chunks

8 ounces jumbo lump crab meat

1 pound black mussels, scrubbed clean, any open mussels discarded

½ cup chopped fresh flat-leaf parsley

¼ cup freshly grated parmesan cheese

THIS SEAFOOD STEW HAS BEEN ONE OF MY FAVORITE *recipes for over a decade. Whenever I find myself making cioppino, I keep coming back to this version of it. I lovingly named it after my friend Jeannie, who shared her beloved recipe with me years ago and let me tinker with it for my low-carb purposes.*

Cioppino is traditionally served with hunks of buttery toasted focaccia. I suggest making the large low-carb croutons from the Low-Carb Panzanella Salad recipe (page 145) to serve with this dish, but it's also superb on its own.

In a Dutch oven or other large pot, heat the olive oil over medium-high heat. Add the fennel, celery, onion, garlic, oregano, and red pepper flakes and season liberally with salt and black pepper. Sauté until the veggies are soft, 10–15 minutes. Turn the heat down to medium-low, add the squid, and cook for 8–10 minutes, stirring occasionally. Add the broth, clam juice, lemon zest, and lemon juice, season again with salt and black pepper, and bring to a boil. Add the tomatoes with their juices and the tomato paste, season once again with salt and black pepper, and bring to a boil. Add the shrimp and cook for 2–3 minutes, until the shrimp are cooked through. Add the fish and crab and cook for 2–3 minutes. Stir in the mussels, cover, and cook for 4–5 minutes, until the mussel shells open. (Discard any mussels that do not open.) Season once more with salt and black pepper. Serve in large bowls garnished with parsley and grated parmesan.

WALNUT BOLOGNESE VEGETABLE STEW

 SERVES 4–6

1½ cups shelled walnut pieces

2 tablespoons olive oil

1 cup finely chopped onion

1 cup finely chopped celery

1 cup shredded carrot

2½ teaspoons salt, divided

½ teaspoon pepper

1 teaspoon dried oregano

1 teaspoon minced garlic

1 cup fresh basil leaves, chopped, divided

1 (14-ounce) can no-sugar-added diced tomatoes

2 tablespoons tomato paste

2 cups water

2 zucchini, quartered lengthwise, then cut crosswise into 1-inch pieces

2 cups quartered baby portobello or cremini mushrooms

1 pound asparagus, trimmed and cut into 1-inch pieces

½ cup canned no-sugar-added coconut cream/milk

THIS HEARTY, SATISFYING VEGETABLE STEW USES *walnuts for the protein. But if you're missing the meat, you could add beef stew meat or ground beef.*

Preheat the oven to 350 degrees F.

Spread out the walnut pieces on a rimmed baking sheet and toast in the oven for 6–8 minutes, or until fragrant. Set aside to cool.

Heat the olive oil in a large saucepan over medium heat until shimmering. Add the onion, celery, and carrot and season with 1 teaspoon of the salt and the pepper. Sauté until the vegetables are tender, 6–8 minutes. Add the oregano, garlic, walnut pieces, and half of the basil. Cook for 3 minutes, then add the tomatoes with their juices and tomato paste. Season with another 1 teaspoon salt and sauté for 10 minutes. Add the water, zucchini, mushrooms, and asparagus. Bring to a boil, cover, and simmer for 1 hour. Add the remaining ½ teaspoon salt, remaining basil, and coconut cream/milk. Simmer, covered, for 20 minutes, then serve.

TOMATO BISQUE

 SERVES 4–6

FOR YEARS, I ROASTED TOMATOES FOR MY TOMATO *soup. Then a chef friend of mine told me she uses my Eat Happy Kitchen Pink Crema sauce to make herself dinner when she comes home from a long night at work. This got me thinking: Why don't I write an easier version of tomato soup so folks can get dinner on the table faster? Hence, this recipe was born.*

In a blender or food processor, combine the marinara, broth, cream, and basil and blend until creamy. Pour the mixture into a large saucepan and heat over medium-low heat. When the soup is hot, ladle into soup bowls and garnish with the pine nuts and dollops of ricotta.

1 (26-ounce) jar Eat Happy Kitchen Tomato Basil Marinara *or* 3 cups Homemade Tomato Basil Marinara (page 30)

1 cup chicken broth

1 cup heavy cream

½ cup packed fresh basil leaves, loosely chopped

2 tablespoons pine nuts, toasted

¼ cup full-fat ricotta cheese, homemade (page 35) or store-bought, drained of excess liquid, if needed

ITALIAN WEDDING SOUP

 SERVES 6–8

MEATBALLS

1 pound ground beef

8 ounces ground mild Italian
    sausage

½ cup freshly grated parmesan
    cheese

1 tablespoon chopped fresh
    chives

1 tablespoon chopped fresh
    oregano leaves

1 tablespoon chopped fresh basil
    leaves

1 teaspoon minced garlic

1 teaspoon salt

½ teaspoon pepper

½ teaspoon onion powder

2 large eggs

SOUP

2 tablespoons olive oil

½ large onion, finely chopped

2 celery stalks, finely chopped

2 carrots, finely chopped

1 teaspoon garlic powder

1 teaspoon salt

½ teaspoon pepper

4–6 cups chicken broth

1 cup cauliflower "rice"

2 cups chopped escarole, kale,
    Swiss chard, or spinach

Freshly grated parmesan cheese,
    for garnish

ITALIAN WEDDING SOUP IS NAMED AFTER A MISUN-
*derstood translation of the Italian word for "to marry," as
it refers to the flavors in the soup "marrying." Yet this has
become a special occasion soup, and we always have it
on Thanksgiving and Christmas (but not at weddings, as
that would be messy). My husband's Aunt Phyllis is known
to make the best Italian wedding soup in the family, but
please don't tell her that I'm not using any pasta in my
version.*

Preheat the oven to 400 degrees F. Line a rimmed
baking sheet with parchment paper.

Combine all the meatball ingredients in a large bowl
and mix well by hand. Form the mixture into 1-inch
balls and place them on the prepared baking sheet.
Bake for 12–15 minutes, or until cooked through.

To make the soup, in a Dutch oven or other large pot,
heat the olive oil over medium-high heat until shimmering. Add the onion, celery, and carrots and cook
until soft, 3–4 minutes. Season with the garlic powder, salt, and pepper and cook for 1–2 more minutes.
Add the broth and cauliflower rice and bring to a boil.
Add the meatballs and simmer for 8–10 minutes, until
meatballs start to cook through. Add the escarole and
simmer for 3–4 minutes, until it softens. Taste and
season once more with salt and pepper if needed. If you
can, keep the heat on low for 10–15 minutes to let the
flavors marry (hence the name "wedding" soup). If you
can't, serve immediately to the hungry masses, garnished with fresh parmesan.

TUSCAN BEAN SOUP

 SERVES 6–8

ONE OF THE MOST WONDERFUL USES OF WHITE
beans is this Tuscan-style soup. The pancetta gives it a
savory depth that complements the white beans and veg-
gies. The longer this soup can simmer, the better!

I n a Dutch oven or other large pot, cook the pancetta
over medium-high heat until translucent, 3–4 minutes. Add the onion, celery, and carrot and cook until
soft, 3–4 minutes. Add the garlic and cook for 1–2 minutes, until fragrant. Season with salt and pepper. Toss
in the oregano and thyme sprigs and give them a
quick stir.

Push the veggies to the outer rim of the pot. Add
¼ cup of the beans to the center. Using the back of a
wooden spoon or ladle, mash the beans into a paste
and stir it in with the vegetables. Pour in the remaining
beans and the broth. Bring the soup to a boil and add
the chard. Season with salt and pepper. Reduce the
heat to medium-low and simmer for 15–20 minutes.
Taste the soup and season with more salt and pepper if
needed. Serve garnished with grated parmesan.

¼ cup chopped pancetta

1 onion, chopped

3 celery stalks, chopped

1 carrot, chopped

2 garlic cloves, minced

Salt and pepper

3 oregano sprigs

3 thyme sprigs

1 (15-ounce) can great northern or
cannellini beans, drained and
rinsed, divided

4 cups chicken broth

1 bunch Swiss chard, chopped

Freshly grated parmesan cheese,
for garnish

CREAMY SAUSAGE PESTO SOUP

 SERVES 4–6

1 pound mild Italian sausage links

2 tablespoons olive oil

1 large leek, white and palest
   green parts only, thinly sliced
   crosswise

2 carrots, sliced

1 cup thinly sliced white button,
   baby portobello, or cremini
   mushrooms

Salt and pepper

1 teaspoon onion powder

1 teaspoon garlic powder

4 cups chicken broth

1 bunch kale, stems removed,
   leaves chopped

½ cup heavy cream

1 cup basil pesto, homemade
   (page 27) or store-bought

I LOVE BROTHY STEWS, BUT THEY'VE GOTTA HAVE *some heft to them if you're going to spend the time in the kitchen, I'd say. This recipe has heartiness to spare. To save some time, you can use jarred pesto for the garnish. If you are using salted broth, you won't need to add much salt to this soup. But if you use store-bought unsalted broth, definitely taste the soup as it goes along and add more salt as you see fit.*

In a large, flat-bottomed sauté pan, cook the sausage links over medium-high heat until brown, 5–7 minutes. Transfer the sausage to a cutting board and let cool for 5 minutes. Cut the sausage into ½-inch-thick disks. Return the sausage to the pan and brown each side over medium-high heat, 1–2 minutes. Transfer the sausage to a paper towel–lined plate to drain.

In a Dutch oven or other large pot, heat the oil over medium-high heat until shimmering. Add the leek, carrots, and mushrooms and cook for 2–3 minutes. Season with salt and pepper, then stir in the onion powder and garlic powder. Pour in the chicken broth and bring to a boil. Add the sausage, then reduce the heat and simmer for 8–10 minutes. Stir in the kale and cook for 5–7 minutes. Season with salt and pepper to taste. Turn off the heat and stir in the heavy cream.

Serve in bowls garnished with a large dollop of pesto sauce.

FAVA BEAN SOUP

 SERVES 2–3

FAVA BEANS ARE ONLY IN SEASON ONCE A YEAR IN *late spring, so take advantage and overbuy these delicious legumes. Three pounds of fava bean pods yields about two cups of beans, so be sure to buy more pods if you want to increase the yield of this recipe. Using a blender will whip a lot of air into the soup and make it almost frothy. If you'd like to cut the frothiness, you can add more chicken broth.*

Salt and pepper

3 pounds fava beans, shelled

1 tablespoon olive oil, plus more for drizzling

¼ sweet onion, roughly chopped

1 cup chicken or vegetable broth

¼ cup heavy cream

Bring a large pot of salted water to a boil. Add the fava beans and blanch for 2–3 minutes, or until they turn bright green and slightly tender. Drain and let cool enough to be able to remove the waxy skin from the beans and discard. Set the beans aside.

In a large nonstick sauté pan, heat the olive oil over medium-high heat until shimmering. Add the onion and cook until soft and fragrant, 3–4 minutes. Season with salt and pepper. Add the broth and heat until warm. Season again with salt and pepper.

Put the fava beans in a blender and season with salt and pepper. Add the onion mixture and puree until smooth. Add the cream, season once more with salt and pepper, and pulse until blended. Serve immediately, drizzled with extra olive oil.

ROASTED BUTTERNUT LASAGNA STEW

 SERVES 3–4

BUTTERNUT SQUASH "NOODLES"

1 butternut squash

Olive oil, for drizzling

Salt and pepper

½ teaspoon garlic powder

½ teaspoon dried oregano

½ teaspoon dried basil

6 garlic cloves, peeled

LASAGNA STEW

1 pound ground beef

½ medium sweet onion, diced

2 tablespoons finely grated carrot

½ teaspoon garlic powder

½ teaspoon onion powder

½ teaspoon salt

¼ teaspoon pepper

1 (26-ounce) jar Eat Happy Kitchen Tomato Basil Marinara or 3 cups Homemade Tomato Basil Marinara (page 30)

¼ cup beef or chicken broth

¼ cup chopped fresh basil, plus more for garnish

1 cup full-fat ricotta cheese, homemade (page 35) or store-bought

½ cup freshly grated parmesan cheese

I'VE SEEN MANY SOUPS AND STEWS WITH TORN *pieces of pasta or even ravioli. Why do the pasta eaters get to have all the fun? You can use butternut squash to replicate the flat shape of ravioli, add beef and sauce, and garnish with lots of ricotta and parmesan for a deconstructed lasagna stew that's to die for.*

Preheat the oven to 350 degrees F. Line a rimmed baking sheet with parchment paper.

To make the butternut squash "noodles," microwave the butternut squash for 1–2 minutes to make cutting the squash easier. Carefully cut away the squash peel and discard it. Cut the squash in half and scoop out and discard the seeds. Then, thinly slice the squash into 2-inch square pieces. Lay the squash pieces in a single layer on the prepared baking sheet and drizzle with olive oil. Season well with salt and pepper and the garlic powder, oregano, and basil. Scatter the garlic cloves around the butternut squash. Bake for 25–30 minutes, until the squash "noodles" are soft and starting to crisp on the edges but not burned.

To make the lasagna stew, in a large, flat-bottomed sauté pan, brown the ground beef and onion over medium-high heat until the beef is cooked through and the onion is soft, stirring with a spatula to break up the meat. Stir in the carrot, garlic powder, onion powder, salt, and pepper. Pour in the marinara and broth. Stir to combine, then bring just to a boil. Reduce the heat and fold in the basil, butternut squash "noodles," and roasted garlic cloves (if desired).

Ladle into bowls and garnish with additional chopped basil, a dollop of ricotta, and grated parmesan.

LASAGNA BOLOGNESE WITH CABBAGE LEAVES

 SERVES 8–10

1 head green cabbage, core discarded and leaves carefully
separated

2 tablespoons olive oil

1 onion, chopped

¼ cup finely grated carrot

2 teaspoons minced garlic

1 pound ground beef

1 pound ground mild Italian
sausage

1½ (26-ounce) jars Eat Happy
Kitchen Tomato Basil Mar-
inara or 4 cups Homemade
Tomato Basil Marinara
(page 30)

1½ cups full-fat ricotta cheese,
home-made (page 35) or store-
bought

1 cup freshly grated parmesan
cheese

3 large eggs

2 tablespoons chopped fresh flat-
leaf parsley

1 (8-ounce) ball fresh mozzarella
cheese, patted dry and thinly
sliced

FOR THIS LASAGNA, WE USE CABBAGE LEAVES IN
*place of noodles for something a little different. Use jarred
sauce for a shortcut, or you can make your own. I also like
to make my own ricotta (page 35).*

Preheat the oven to 350 degrees F.

Bring a large pot of water to a boil. Add the cabbage
leaves and cook for 4–5 minutes, until pliable but not
tearing. Carefully remove them from the water and lay
them on clean kitchen towels to cool off and dry. Blot
any excess water from the leaves with a towel. When
cool enough to handle, cut out any rough stems from
the center of the leaves and discard. Cut the remaining
leaves into 3-inch pieces. Continue to blot dry if the
leaves release more water.

In a large, flat-bottomed nonstick sauté pan, heat
the olive oil over medium-high heat. Add the onion and
cook until soft, 4–5 minutes. Add the carrot and garlic
and cook for 2 minutes.

Add the ground beef and sausage and cook, using
a spatula to chop the meat into smaller pieces, until
browned and cooked through, 4–5 minutes. Drain off
the excess grease. Add the marinara and stir to mix.
Turn the heat down to low and simmer.

In a large bowl, whisk together the ricotta, parmesan,
eggs, and parsley until creamy and smooth.

To assemble the lasagna, spoon one-third of the
meat mixture into a 9 × 13-inch baking pan. Lay down
half of the cabbage leaves on top of the meat. Spread
half of the ricotta mixture evenly over the leaves. Lay
out half of the mozzarella slices on top of the ricotta.

Repeat with another layer of meat, cabbage leaves, and ricotta mixture, then top with the remaining meat and mozzarella.

Bake for 30–45 minutes, or until the lasagna is bubbling and the cheese is melted. Remove from the oven and let stand for at least 10 minutes. Carefully cut it into squares and serve.

STUFFED MANICOTTI

 SERVES 2–3

ONCE I FIGURED OUT HOW TO MAKE LOW-CARB
pasta shells, manicotti was a given. I love to make mani-
cotti with arrabbiata sauce to keep it spicy, but the recipe
is written here with regular marinara. It's delicious and is
sure to cure any baked pasta dish craving.

Preheat the oven to 350 degrees F. Grease a 9 × 13-
inch dish with olive oil.

In a food processor, blend all the pasta shell ingredients into a smooth batter.

Heat 1 teaspoon olive oil in a small nonstick skillet
over medium-high heat until shimmering. Pour ¼ cup
of the batter into the pan and use a spatula to spread
the batter into a 4–6-inch circle. Cover and cook for 2–3
minutes, until cooked through like a crepe. Transfer
the pasta shell to a sheet of parchment paper. Repeat
with the remaining batter to make the rest of the pasta
shells, adding more oil as needed.

To make the filling, in a medium bowl, combine 1¼
cups of the mozzarella, the ricotta, parmesan, spinach,
salt, and pepper and mix with a fork. Add the egg and
mix well.

Spoon about ¼ cup of the cheese-spinach mixture
onto a pasta shell, then roll up the shell and place it seam
side down in the prepared baking dish. Repeat until the
pasta shells and cheese-spinach mixture are used up.

Spoon some marinara sauce around the edges of the
pan, then sprinkle some over the pasta shells. Top with
the remaining ½ cup mozzarella. Bake for 25 minutes,
or until light brown and bubbly. Remove the dish from
the oven, let it stand for 5 minutes, then serve garnished with chopped oregano or basil.

LOW-CARB PASTA SHELLS

Olive oil, for greasing and frying

¼ cup cream cheese, at room
temperature

2 tablespoons salted butter, at
room temperature

3 large eggs plus 1 large egg yolk

¼ cup almond flour

¼ teaspoon salt

¼ teaspoon garlic powder

¼ teaspoon onion powder

FILLING

1¾ cups shredded mozzarella
cheese, divided

1¼ cups full-fat ricotta cheese,
homemade (page 35) or store-
bought

1 cup freshly grated parmesan
cheese

1 cup finely chopped spinach

1 teaspoon salt

½ teaspoon pepper

1 large egg, beaten

1 (26-ounce) jar Eat Happy
Kitchen Tomato Basil Mar-
inara *or* 3 cups Homemade
Tomato Basil Marinara
(page 30)

Chopped fresh oregano or basil
leaves, for garnish

VERDURE E CONTORNI

Vegetables and side dishes shine brightly in this chapter. I indicate when some veggies are only available in certain seasons, but most of these items can be found in American grocery stores year-round. Buy what looks fresh, but it's also a great idea to have a bag or two of cauliflower "rice" on hand to be able to whip up any number of recipes in this book.

Roasted Gorgonzola Leeks and Green Beans, page 153

LOW-CARB PANZANELLA SALAD

 SERVES 6–8

THIS RECIPE USES A VERSION OF MY EASY GRAIN-*free bread recipe to make low-carb croutons. This is a fun way to make a bread salad without feeling like you're missing out on the bread. Because you're not! You're welcome.*

To make the croutons, preheat the oven to 300 degrees F. Lightly grease a rimmed baking sheet with olive oil.

In a large bowl, combine the almond flour, salt, baking soda, eggs, and vinegar and mix well until a thick dough forms. Press the dough flat on the prepared baking sheet to a ¾-inch thickness. Bake on the bottom rack of the oven for 15–20 minutes, until cooked through (the outside of the loaf will be golden brown). Remove the sheet from the oven and let cool completely. Using a pizza cutter or knife, cut into 2-inch squares.

In a large, flat-bottomed nonstick sauté pan or cast-iron skillet, heat 2 tablespoons olive oil over medium-high heat. Working in batches, toast the croutons until browned on both sides, 1–2 minutes per side. Repeat, adding more olive oil to the pan, until all the croutons are toasted. Season the hot croutons with salt. Set aside to cool.

In a small bowl, whisk together all the dressing ingredients.

To make the salad, in a large salad bowl, combine the arugula, bell pepper, parsley, red onion, cucumber, tomatoes, and half of the croutons. Toss with half of the dressing. Spread out the remaining croutons on a large platter. Drizzle with the remaining dressing, then mound the salad atop the croutons. Garnish with mozzarella balls and parmesan, if desired. Serve immediately.

GRAIN-FREE CROUTONS

Olive oil, as needed

2½ cups almond flour

1 teaspoon salt, plus more to taste

½ teaspoon baking soda

3 large eggs

1 teaspoon apple cider vinegar

DRESSING

½ cup olive oil

¼ cup red wine vinegar

1 teaspoon anchovy paste

½ teaspoon garlic powder

½ teaspoon dried oregano

½ teaspoon salt

¼ teaspoon pepper

PANZANELLA SALAD

3–4 cups arugula

1 red bell pepper, cored and thinly sliced

8–10 flat-leaf parsley sprigs

¼ red onion, thinly sliced

½ cucumber, thinly sliced

½ cup halved cherry tomatoes

Mini mozzarella balls (*ciliegine*), for garnish (optional)

Grated fresh parmesan cheese, for garnish (optional)

SPINACH, PEPPERS, AND HERB-TOASTED PINE NUTS

 SERVES 2–3

2 tablespoons olive oil, divided

¼ cup pine nuts

1 tablespoon minced fresh rosemary leaves, divided

1 tablespoon chopped fresh basil leaves, divided

1 shallot, finely chopped

1 red bell pepper, cored and chopped

Salt and pepper

3 cups packed baby spinach

Freshly grated parmesan cheese, for garnish (optional)

I LOVE A QUICK SIDE DISH WITH FRESH INGREDIENTS. *This recipe is perfect to go with summer grilled meats like Bistecca alla Fiorentina (page 100) or a slow-cooked braised meat like Osso Buco (page 108). Note that the 3 cups of spinach will cook down quite a bit, so you are welcome to double the recipe to serve more people.*

Heat 1 tablespoon of the olive oil in a large, flat-bottomed sauté pan over medium-high heat. Add the pine nuts and toast, tossing frequently, until fragrant and starting to brown, 4–5 minutes. In the final minute of toasting, add half each of the rosemary and basil and toss to coat the pine nuts. Transfer the pine nuts to a paper towel–lined plate to drain.

In the same pan, heat the remaining 1 tablespoon olive oil over medium-high heat. Add the shallot and bell pepper and cook for 3–4 minutes. Season with salt and pepper. Stir and cook for an additional 3–4 minutes, until soft, then mix in the remaining rosemary and basil. Cook for 2–3 more minutes, then add the packed spinach. Use tongs to toss the spinach as it heats and wilts, mixing it with the peppers and shallots, until the spinach is fully cooked, 2–3 minutes. Season once more with salt and pepper. Add the herb-toasted pine nuts and toss evenly. Serve immediately, topped with fresh parmesan, if desired.

ZUCCHINI WITH BASIL AND PANCETTA

 SERVES 2–3

WHEN YOU GET BORED OF MAKING THE SAME OL'
*steamed vegetables for your weeknight meals, remember
that this recipe exists. It's quick to make and so flavorful,
which is how you make it to legendary status in the kitchen
while making a humble weeknight dinner that everyone
loves.*

Heat the olive oil in a large, flat-bottomed sauté
pan over medium-high heat. Add the onion
and pancetta and cook until the onion is soft and the
pancetta is browned, 4–6 minutes. Add the zucchini,
garlic powder, salt, pepper, and half of the basil and
toss to coat. Cover, turn the heat down to medium-low,
and cook for 7–9 minutes, until the zucchini is cooked
through but not mushy. Toss again and serve garnished
with the remaining basil.

1 tablespoon olive oil

1 medium sweet onion, sliced

4 ounces pancetta, chopped

2 zucchini, trimmed and cut into
1 × ½-inch pieces

½ teaspoon garlic powder

½ teaspoon salt

¼ teaspoon pepper

¼ cup packed fresh basil leaves,
chopped, divided

CAULIFLOWER RICE WITH ROSEMARY AND PANCETTA

 SERVES 2–3

¼ cup olive oil

2 garlic cloves, thinly sliced

2 teaspoons finely chopped fresh rosemary leaves, plus more for garnish

12 ounces pancetta or bacon, thinly sliced

2 cups cauliflower "rice"

1 tablespoon white wine vinegar

½ cup freshly grated parmesan cheese

Pepper

THIS SAVORY SIDE DISH COMBINES SOME OF MY *favorite Italian flavors, plus it utilizes the delightful fat and salt from pancetta to make it all work together.*

Heat the olive oil in a large, flat-bottomed sauté pan over medium-high heat. Add the garlic and cook until fragrant, 1–2 minutes. Add the rosemary and cook until fragrant, 1–2 minutes. Add the pancetta and cook, tossing frequently, until it's browned but not crisp, 4–5 minutes. Add the cauliflower and toss well. Sprinkle in the vinegar and let it sizzle. Turn the heat down to medium-low and cook, stirring only once or twice, until the cauliflower is cooked through and most of the excess water evaporates, 10–12 minutes. Stir in the fresh parmesan and serve immediately, seasoned with plenty of pepper and additional rosemary.

CAULIFLOWER MASH POLENTA

 YIELDS 1½ CUPS

2 cups cauliflower "rice"

2 tablespoons salted butter

2 tablespoons heavy cream

2 tablespoons sour cream

½ teaspoon garlic powder

Salt and pepper

¼ cup freshly grated parmesan or Grana Padano cheese

THE CREAMINESS OF POLENTA GOES WITH SO MANY *braised meats, it's no wonder that it's the comfort food of northern Italy and a favorite here in the States too. However, giving up grains means we're not using corn, so our trusty friend cauliflower steps in to the rescue. I use this recipe whenever I need to get either a polenta or mashed potato feel, and it's perfect to serve with Osso Buco (page 108) or alongside the Northern Italian Beef Roast (page 107) or Porchetta (page 118).*

Put the cauliflower rice in a large bowl and microwave on high for 3 minutes. Divide the cauliflower evenly between two clean kitchen towels and spread it all out. Press the excess water out of the cauliflower, let it stand for 10 minutes, then press some more. Transfer the cauliflower to a Vitamix or other strong blender, along with the butter, heavy cream, sour cream, garlic powder, and salt and pepper to taste. Pulse the food processor and use the tamper to mash the contents into a firm purée. Open the lid, scrape down the sides, and add the grated parmesan. Close again and pulse a few more times to blend to the desired texture and thickness. Season with salt and pepper once more, if needed, and serve.

ROASTED GORGONZOLA LEEKS AND GREEN BEANS

 SERVES 3–4

IN LATE SUMMER, WHEN STONE FRUITS ARE IN SEA-
*son, I look forward to this side dish. You can use plums,
peaches, pluots, or apricots. This dish pairs perfectly with
roasts or anything from the grill.*

Preheat the oven to 400 degrees F.
Bring a large pot of salted water to a boil. Fill a
large bowl with cold water and ice cubes. Add the
green beans to the boiling water and blanch for 2 minutes, then plunge them into the ice bath for 3 minutes
to stop the cooking process. Transfer to paper towels
to dry.

Drizzle a bit of olive oil in a casserole dish or roasting pan, then lay out the leeks and green beans. Season
well with salt and black pepper. Scatter the olives and
plum slices around the casserole dish. Sprinkle with
red pepper flakes, if desired. Drizzle the entire contents
once more with olive oil. Roast for 25–30 minutes, until
the green beans and leeks are soft. Remove the pan
from the oven and sprinkle the gorgonzola crumbles
and pistachios all over the dish. Put the dish back in the
oven and roast for 5 more minutes. Serve.

Pictured on page 142

1 pound green beans, trimmed

Olive oil, for drizzling

2–3 large leeks, white and palest
green parts only, sliced lengthwise

Salt and black pepper

¼ cup pitted kalamata olives

1 plum, pitted and sliced

½ teaspoon red pepper flakes
(optional)

⅓ cup crumbled gorgonzola
cheese

⅓ cup shelled pistachios

ASPARAGUS CACIO E PEPE

 SERVES 2–3

1 pound asparagus, trimmed and cut into 1-inch pieces

2 tablespoons olive oil

1 tablespoon salted butter

½ cup freshly grated parmesan cheese

½ teaspoon pepper

THIS IS THE FINAL RECIPE OF THE FOUR ROMAN PAS-
*tas referenced in the Primi Piatti chapter. We're going
to pair the simple elegance of cacio e pepe (cheese and
pepper) sauce with tender asparagus instead of bucatini
or spaghetti.*

B ring a medium saucepan of water to a boil. Add the
asparagus and blanch for 2–3 minutes, until bright
green and fork-tender. Drain the asparagus in a colan-
der. Put the olive oil and butter in the hot pot and stir
until melted. Return the asparagus to the pot and fold
in the cheese and pepper until evenly mixed. Serve.

PARSLEY VEGGIES

 SERVES 4

YEARS AGO IN ITALY I HAD THE SIMPLEST PREPARA-
*tion of porcini mushrooms in olive oil covered in fresh
parsley. This was at a time when in the States, a sprig of
parsley was used only as a decorative garnish on plates
at restaurants. I had no idea how potent fresh parsley
can be, much less the delight of Italian flat-leaf parsley.
I've tweaked this over the years to add onion and zucchini. I use golden zucchini when in season (pictured
here), which tastes the same as regular zucchini but has
a beautiful yellow color, reminiscent of summer squash.
For mushrooms, you can substitute white button, cremini,
or shiitake mushrooms for the baby portobellos. This is a
versatile dish with herbs at the heart of the flavor profile.
It also is perfect the next day as leftovers scrambled with
eggs and freshly grated parmesan.*

2 tablespoons olive oil

1 sweet onion, thinly sliced

1 pound baby portobello mushrooms or portobello mushroom
caps, thinly sliced

Salt and pepper

2 small green or golden zucchini,
thinly sliced on a mandoline

1 teaspoon garlic powder

½ cup chopped fresh flat-leaf
parsley

⅓ cup chopped fresh basil

Heat the olive oil in a large, flat-bottomed sauté
pan over medium-high heat. Add the onion and
cook until soft and starting to sear, 3–4 minutes. Add
the mushrooms and toss, let them sear for 1–2 minutes,
then toss again to sear most sides of the mushrooms,
another 1–2 minutes. Cook for 3–4 more minutes, or
until the mushrooms start to soften and get cooked
through. Season with salt and pepper. Add the zucchini
and garlic powder and toss well. Season again with salt
and pepper, reduce the heat to low, cover, and simmer for 6–8 minutes, until the zucchini is soft but not
mushy. Toss in the parsley and basil and serve.

BRAISED FENNEL AND SHALLOTS

 SERVES 2–3

2 pounds fennel bulbs

2 tablespoons olive oil

2 shallots, sliced lengthwise

Juice of ½ lemon (about 1 tablespoon)

Salt and pepper

¼ cup chicken broth

1 star anise pod

BRAISED FENNEL IS THE PERFECT SIDE DISH TO GO *with rich stews and roasts, or to serve alongside fish or shellfish. Try replacing the lemon in this recipe with another citrus that's in season, such as blood orange or Meyer lemon.*

———————————————

Trim the fennel fronds; chop and reserve a handful of the fronds and discard the remaining fronds. Trim and discard the bottoms of the fennel bulbs. Slice the bulbs lengthwise into quarters.

Heat the olive oil in a large, flat-bottomed sauté pan over medium-high heat until shimmering. Add the fennel bulbs and sear for 2–3 minutes. Add the shallots and cook for 1–2 minutes. Add the lemon juice and let it sizzle. Season well with salt and pepper. Turn the heat down to medium-low and add the broth and star anise. Cover and simmer for 10–12 minutes, until the fennel and shallots are fork-tender. Toss in the chopped fronds and cook for 2–3 minutes. Remove and discard the star anise and serve.

ROASTED ROSEMARY GARLIC RADISHES

 SERVES 2–4

RADISHES ARE A GREAT REPLACEMENT FOR ROASTED *potatoes. They can get bitter upon roasting, so we dredge them in oil, garlic, salt, and rosemary to make them tasty and comforting.*

1–2 pounds radishes, trimmed and halved

3 tablespoons olive oil

1 teaspoon minced garlic

1 teaspoon minced fresh rosemary leaves, plus more for garnish

1 teaspoon salt

½ teaspoon pepper

Preheat the oven to 400 degrees F. Line a rimmed baking sheet with parchment paper.

Toss the radishes on the prepared baking sheet with the olive oil, garlic, rosemary, salt, and pepper. Spread out the coated radishes in a single layer, some face down and some face up, and roast for 25–30 minutes, until the exteriors are wrinkled and the interiors are fork-tender. Remove from the oven and let stand for 10 minutes, then serve, garnished with additional rosemary.

MINTED CHARRED BROCCOLINI

 SERVES 2

1 pound broccolini, rough ends
    trimmed and stalks peeled

1 tablespoon olive oil, plus more
    for drizzling

Salt and pepper

½ cup chopped fresh mint

Lemon wedges, for serving

FRESH, FAST, AND EASY. SOUNDS LIKE THE SLOGAN
*of your local fast-food joint, doesn't it? It's not! It's the
perfect description of this broccolini recipe. I love a seared
vegetable, and the addition of fresh lemon and mint at the
end brightens up the char and wakes up the palate.*

———————————————————————

Bring a large pot of salted water to a boil. Add the
broccolini and boil for 2 minutes, until bright
green. Using tongs or a slotted spoon, transfer to a
paper towel–lined plate to drain.

Heat the olive oil in a large nonstick sauté pan or
cast-iron skillet over high heat. Add the broccolini
and sear for 2–4 minutes, until charred. Transfer to a
serving platter, season with salt and pepper, and serve
garnished with an extra drizzle of olive oil, the chopped
mint, and a squeeze of lemon.

EGGPLANT INVOLTINI

 SERVES 3–4

2–3 large eggplants, trimmed and sliced lengthwise into ½-inch-thick slices

Salt

2 tablespoons olive oil

1½ cups full-fat ricotta cheese, homemade (page 35) or store-bought

1 cup freshly grated parmesan cheese

1 tablespoon grated lemon zest

1 teaspoon fresh thyme leaves

1 teaspoon chopped fresh oregano leaves

½ teaspoon pepper

½ (26-ounce) jar Eat Happy Kitchen Tomato Basil Marinara *or* 1–2 cups Homemade Tomato Basil Marinara (page 30)

7–10 fresh basil leaves, chopped

INVOLTINI MEANS "ROLLS," AND THEY'RE BASICALLY *the same as a braciola, a French roulade, or a German rouladen. Every culture has a delicious rolled-up bundle of goodness, and this is the Italian one using eggplant. You can substitute chicken, pork, or beef (pounded out thinly) for the eggplant if you'd like more protein.*

———————————————

Preheat the oven to 400 degrees F. Line a rimmed baking sheet with parchment paper.

Lay the eggplant slices on paper towels and season both sides with salt. Let the eggplant "sweat" for 10–15 minutes (the salt will draw beads of water out of the eggplant). Blot the eggplant dry with a paper towel.

Transfer the eggplant to the prepared baking sheet, brush with the olive oil, and roast for 7–8 minutes per side, until soft and starting to brown. Let the eggplant cool while you assemble the filling. Leave the oven on.

In a medium bowl, combine the ricotta, parmesan, lemon zest, thyme, oregano, and pepper. Spoon 1–2 heaping tablespoons of the cheese mixture at the bottom edge of an eggplant slice. Roll up the eggplant slice and secure it with a toothpick, if needed. Gently place the eggplant roll-up in a baking dish. Repeat the roll-up process with the remaining cheese mixture and eggplant slices.

Pour the marinara into the baking dish around the eggplant rolls. Bake for 10–15 minutes, until the marinara is bubbling. Remove the dish from the oven, let stand for 5 minutes, then serve garnished with the basil.

Finished Eggplant Involtini pictured on pages 166–167

Eggplant Involtini, recipe page 164

BRUSSELS SPROUTS, MARINARA, AND GUANCIALE

 SERVES 2–4

1 cup chopped guanciale or
    pancetta

1 shallot, diced

1 pound Brussels sprouts,
    trimmed and quartered

Salt and pepper

½ (26-ounce) jar Eat Happy
    Kitchen Tomato Basil Mari-
    nara or 1–2 cups Homemade
    Tomato Basil Marinara
    (page 30)

AS MENTIONED AT THE BEGINNING OF THE PRIMI
*Piatti chapter, guanciale is cured pork jowl and is a deli-
cacy in Italy. You can usually find this in the cured meats
section of the grocery store, but you are welcome to substitute pancetta or bacon if you can't find guanciale.*

*This recipe is a perfect side dish for steak, fish, or
roasts as it complements meat without a lot of fuss. In
other words, easy prep and great flavor (thanks to the
guanciale).*

Heat a large, flat-bottomed sauté pan over medium-high heat. Add the guanciale and cook until crispy, 10–12 minutes. Add the shallot and cook until soft, 3–4 minutes. Add the Brussels sprouts and toss until coated with the shallot-guanciale mixture. Season with salt and pepper. Pour the marinara into the pan and toss. Bring the mixture to a boil, then cover and simmer for 15–20 minutes, until the Brussels sprouts are soft. Stir well and serve.

ROASTED STUFFED TOMATOES

 SERVES 4

IF LIFE FINDS YOU WITH EXTRA TOMATOES FROM THE *garden, or with tomatoes that you overzealously bought from the grocery store, make these stuffed tomatoes. They're a perfect lunch on their own, or a dinner side dish that is rustic fabulousness. Be gentle working with the roasted tomatoes as they can tear easily.*

Preheat the oven to 450 degrees F. Place the tomatoes on a rimmed baking sheet.

Heat the olive oil in a large nonstick sauté pan over medium-high heat. Add the onion and cook until soft and translucent, 3–4 minutes. Add the broccoli, toss, and cook for 2–3 minutes, until the broccoli starts to turn bright green. Add the carrot and parsley and cook for 2–3 minutes. Stir in the garlic, salt, oregano, cumin, and nutmeg. Add the spinach leaves and toss until they're wilted, about 2 minutes. Pour in the marinara and mix thoroughly. Bring to a boil, then remove the pan from the heat.

Fold in the fontina and 2 tablespoons of the almond flour. Scoop the mixture evenly into the hollowed-out tomatoes. Sprinkle ½ tablespoon of the remaining almond flour on each tomato, then drizzle olive oil over the top. Roast for 6–8 minutes, or until the tomatoes are soft and the almond flour topping is starting to brown. Serve.

4 firm beefsteak tomatoes, cored, seeds and innards discarded

1 tablespoon olive oil, plus more for drizzling

½ medium onion, diced

1 cup chopped broccoli florets

¼ cup grated carrot

2 tablespoons chopped fresh flat-leaf parsley

1 teaspoon minced garlic

½ teaspoon salt

½ teaspoon dried oregano

½ teaspoon ground cumin

¼ teaspoon ground nutmeg

1 cup spinach leaves, loosely chopped

1 cup Eat Happy Kitchen Tomato Basil Marinara or Home-made Tomato Basil Marinara (page 30)

½ cup grated fontina cheese

4 tablespoons almond flour, divided

BEEF AND MUSHROOM–STUFFED ZUCCHINI

 SERVES 4–6

4–5 large zucchini, trimmed

Salt and pepper

1 tablespoon olive oil

½ onion, diced

1 pound ground beef

1 cup chopped baby portobello or cremini mushrooms

½ teaspoon garlic powder

½ teaspoon onion powder

½ teaspoon dried oregano

1 (26-ounce) jar Eat Happy Kitchen Tomato Basil Marinara or 2–3 cups Homemade Tomato Basil Marinara (page 30)

1 cup shredded mozzarella cheese

THIS FILLING SIDE DISH COULD BE A MEAL ON ITS *own. It's also a fun and delicious way to get the young folks in the house to eat their meat and vegetables by calling them zucchini boats. I don't know why we think we can trick kids by using cute names for things, but sometimes it works, and you get the fam eating things they might not otherwise.*

Preheat the oven to 350 degrees F. Cut the zucchini in half lengthwise, then scoop out and discard the innards, leaving a ½-inch-thick shell. Lay the zucchini halves on a rimmed baking sheet and season with salt and pepper. Let the zucchini "sweat" (the salt will draw beads of water out of the zucchini) for 10–15 minutes while you prepare the filling.

Heat the olive oil in a large sauté pan over medium-high heat. Add the onion and cook until soft, 3–4 minutes. Add the ground beef and cook, breaking up the beef with a spatula, until browned, 4–5 minutes. Add the mushrooms and cook for 4–5 minutes, until they start to soften. Season the beef and mushrooms liberally with salt and pepper, then stir in the garlic powder, onion powder, and oregano. Fold in the marinara and cook until heated through.

Blot the zucchini dry with a paper towel. Bake the zucchini for 10 minutes. Remove the zucchini from the oven and scoop the meat mixture into each zucchini. Bake for 15 more minutes. Remove the zucchini from the oven and top with the mozzarella cheese. Bake for 5–8 minutes, or until the zucchini is soft to the touch and the cheese is melted and bubbly. Serve.

BREAKFAST

In old-school Italian cookbooks, there is nary a breakfast chapter to be found. I'm not going to lie; my old country brethren are not fans of big breakfasts. Instead they love a hard roll or pastry. If you are old-school (or if you like to fast until lunch), then you are welcome to ignore what a lot of Americans consider the most important meal of the day. For the rest of us who love breakfast, I present to y'all some delicious breakfast dishes with Italian flavor twists. Some are quick to make for a weekday morning, some work as light lunches or "breakfast for dinner" meals. A few recipes take longer to prepare, and I hope these become your new favorite brunch dishes.

Basil Zucchini Frittata (left), page 182, and Lemon Ricotta Pancakes (right), page 181

ITALIAN EGGS BENEDICT

 SERVES 3–6

EVERY TIME I GO TO ITALY, I HAVE LOTS OF COFFEE *for breakfast, but no brunch. I don't know if there's any such thing as an Italian brunch. But we love brunch here in America, and we shouldn't be stopped from enjoying Italian flavors as a part of our brunch tradition. Plus, you can always make a Bellini or a mimosa with prosecco to add more Italian flair to your brunch table.*

To make the muffin baskets, preheat the oven to 400 degrees F. Spray 6 cups of a muffin tin with olive oil spray.

In a large bowl, combine all the muffin ingredients and form into a dough ball. Divide the ball into 6 equal parts and press them into the 6 prepared muffin cups, leaving an indentation in each muffin to hold an egg. Bake for 15–20 minutes, until golden brown and cooked through. Set aside.

To make the eggs Benedict, cook the pancetta in a small sauté pan over medium-high heat until crispy. Transfer the pancetta to a paper towel–lined plate to drain.

Fill a large saucepan with water, add the vinegar, and bring to a boil. One by one, carefully crack the eggs into the boiling water and poach for 3–4 minutes for medium doneness. Using a slotted spoon, transfer the eggs to a paper towel–lined plate to drain.

In a blender, blend the basil, parmesan, olive oil, pine nuts, and garlic until you've reached your desired pesto texture. Season with salt and pepper to taste.

To assemble, place the muffin baskets on serving plates. Add a scoop of burrata to each muffin. Season with salt and pepper and drizzle with olive oil. Place an egg on top. Top the egg with pesto and pancetta. Add arugula leaves and cherry tomatoes to each plate. Serve.

LOW-CARB MUFFIN BASKETS

Olive oil spray

1½ cups shredded mozzarella cheese

1 large egg

3 tablespoons cream cheese, at room temperature

2 tablespoons finely chopped sun-dried tomatoes

¾ cup almond flour

½ teaspoon garlic powder

½ teaspoon dried basil

ITALIAN EGGS BENEDICT

¼ cup chopped pancetta

2 tablespoons white vinegar

6 large eggs

1 cup packed fresh basil leaves

¼ cup freshly grated parmesan cheese

2 tablespoons olive oil, plus more for drizzling

1 tablespoon pine nuts or chopped walnuts

1 teaspoon minced garlic

Salt and pepper

1 (8-ounce) ball burrata cheese, divided

Arugula, for serving

¼ cup chopped cherry tomatoes, for serving

MUSHROOMS AND PANCETTA WITH SHERRY CREAM SAUCE AND POACHED EGGS

 SERVES 2

½ cup chopped pancetta

2 cups thinly sliced white button or cremini mushrooms

Juice of 1 lemon (about 2 tablespoons)

2 tablespoons sherry vinegar or white wine vinegar

1 cup heavy cream

½ teaspoon salt

¼ teaspoon pepper

4 large eggs

6 cups water

2 tablespoons white vinegar

1 tablespoon finely chopped fresh chives

THIS BREAKFAST DISH COMBINES MY FAVORITE *taste sensations: the heartiness of mushrooms, the umami of pancetta, the acidity of sherry, and the smoothness of cream and egg yolks. This is a special weekend brunch dish that's actually quick to cook, but it tastes like decadent heaven.*

Heat a large, flat-bottomed sauté pan over medium-high heat. Add the pancetta and cook until crispy, 3–5 minutes. Transfer the pancetta to a paper towel–lined plate to drain, leaving the fat in the pan.

Add the mushrooms to the pan and cook until soft, 3–4 minutes. Add the lemon juice and sherry vinegar, then immediately stir in the heavy cream. Bring to a boil, then reduce the heat to a simmer. Stir in the salt and pepper and cook, stirring often, for 6–8 minutes, until the sauce starts to thicken.

Meanwhile, fill a large saucepan with water, add the white vinegar, and bring to a boil. One by one, carefully crack the eggs into the boiling water and poach for 3–4 minutes for medium doneness. Using a slotted spoon, transfer the eggs to a paper towel–lined plate to drain.

Add the pancetta to the mushroom-sherry-cream mixture and stir well. Divide the mixture onto serving plates, then top with the poached eggs. Garnish with the chives and serve immediately.

LEMON RICOTTA PANCAKES

 YIELDS 7–8 LARGE PANCAKES

CAN YOU HAVE A PANCAKE WITHOUT SUGARS AND *grains that actually tastes good without syrup? Don't make me come over there and slap the fake keto maple syrup out of your hand. The answer is a resounding yes! All my books have great pancake recipes in them because low-carb humans might want to branch out from eggs from time to time.*

These lemon ricotta pancakes are light, fresh, and airy with just a hint of lemon. Yet somehow, if you eat 3 or 4 of them, you will be incredibly full. Lemon plus ricotta is a traditional Italian flavor combination that can be used in a number of ways, but the pancake might just be the perfect application. You can cook them in salted butter if you like, but there's just something about sweet cream butter that brings out the best in these simple pancakes. Feel free to make your own ricotta (page 35).

¾ cup full-fat ricotta cheese, homemade (page 35) or store-bought

½ cup almond flour

1 teaspoon grated lemon zest, plus more for garnish

Juice of ½ lemon (about 1 table-spoon)

¼ teaspoon salt

3 large eggs

½ teaspoon baking soda

Unsalted butter, for frying

In a large bowl, stir together the ricotta, almond flour, lemon zest, lemon juice, and salt. Add the eggs and whisk until smooth. Whisk in the baking soda.

Heat 1–2 tablespoons butter in a large, flat-bottomed nonstick sauté pan over medium-high heat until the butter is bubbling and coating the pan. Working in batches, scoop ¼ cup of the batter into the pan. As the batter heats up, the pancakes will flatten, but you can use a spatula to flatten them if you need to. Cook for 2–3 minutes, tilting the pan periodically to allow the butter to cook the sides of the pancakes, until the bottom of the pancake is browned. Flip the pancakes and cook on the other side for 1 minute. Repeat to cook the remaining pancakes, adding more butter as needed.

Transfer the pancakes to serving plates, garnish with additional lemon zest, and serve.

BASIL ZUCCHINI FRITTATA

 SERVES 2–3

6 large eggs

2 tablespoons heavy cream

Salt and pepper

½ cup packed fresh basil leaves, chopped

2 tablespoons salted butter

1 tablespoon olive oil

1 shallot, chopped

½ cup chopped zucchini

Freshly grated parmesan cheese, for garnish (optional)

THE FOLLOWING TWO RECIPES ARE FOR THE CLASSIC *Italian egg dish, the blessed frittata. I love to make fritta-tas with any leftover vegetables from the previous night's dinner, or just to use up any vegetables, shallots, and herbs that might otherwise go to waste. This recipe uses a cast-iron skillet only because you need to soften the shal-lot and zucchini on the stovetop before transferring the pan to the oven. If you do not have an oven-safe skillet, you can cook the shallot and zucchini and then transfer them to a casserole dish for baking the frittata.*

Preheat the oven to 350 degrees F.
Beat the eggs and cream in a medium bowl until pale yellow. Season well with salt and pepper. Fold in the basil and set aside.

Heat the butter and olive oil in a large cast-iron skillet over medium-high heat until shimmering and starting to bubble. Add the shallot and cook until soft, 1–2 minutes. Add the zucchini and cook until soft, 3–4 minutes. Season with salt and pepper.

Pour the egg mixture into the pan. As soon as the edges start to firm up, transfer the pan to the oven and bake for 15 minutes, or until cooked through. Serve im-mediately, garnished with grated parmesan, if you like.

SPICY CALABRIAN FRITTATA

 SERVES 3–4

6–8 large eggs

2 tablespoons heavy cream

Salt and pepper

½ cup chopped roasted red bell pepper and/or other chopped cooked vegetables

1 teaspoon chopped Calabrian hot peppers or chopped dried hot peppers

2 tablespoons salted butter

1 tablespoon olive oil

3 tablespoons goat cheese

CALABRIAN CHILES ARE SPICIER THAN JALAPENOS *and have a bright, fruity flavor. This flexible recipe is a great way to use up other leftover cooked vegetables in addition to the peppers and can be made either in a cast-iron skillet or a casserole dish.*

Cast-Iron Skillet Instructions:

Preheat the oven to 350 degrees F.

Beat the eggs and cream in a medium bowl until pale yellow. Season well with salt and pepper. Fold in the roasted red peppers and Calabrian hot peppers and set aside.

Heat the butter and olive oil in a large cast-iron skillet over medium-high heat until shimmering and starting to bubble. Pour in the egg mixture. As soon as the edges start to firm up, crumble the goat cheese on top, transfer the pan to the oven, and bake for 15 minutes, or until cooked through. Serve immediately.

Casserole Dish Instructions:

Preheat the oven to 350 degrees F.

Put the olive oil and butter in an 8 × 8-inch or 7 × 9-inch casserole dish. Heat in the oven for 5–6 minutes, until the casserole dish is warm and the butter is melting. Remove the dish from the oven and gently shake it around to coat the bottom with the oil and butter.

Beat the eggs and cream in a medium bowl until pale yellow. Season well with salt and pepper. Fold in the roasted red peppers and Calabrian hot peppers, then pour the mixture into the casserole dish. Crumble the goat cheese over the top and bake for 15 minutes, or until cooked through. Serve immediately.

HAM AND CHEESE CLOUD EGGS

 SERVES 2–3

THIS IS A FUN TREND IN THE LOW-CARB MOVEMENT *and a cute presentation for eggs. I gave these eggs an Italian twist with the addition of prosciutto, fresh basil, and two Italian cheeses.*

2–3 slices prosciutto

6 large eggs, separated

½ teaspoon salt

½ teaspoon garlic powder

¼ teaspoon onion powder

¼ teaspoon pepper

⅓ cup grated fontina cheese

½ cup freshly grated parmesan cheese

7–10 fresh basil leaves, chopped

Preheat the oven to 425 degrees F. Line a rimmed baking sheet with parchment paper.

Fry the prosciutto slices in a small sauté pan over medium-high heat until crispy, about 2 minutes. Transfer to a paper towel to drain.

In a medium bowl, beat the egg whites, salt, garlic powder, onion powder, and pepper with a hand mixer until stiff peaks form, about 2 minutes. Scoop six even portions of the egg whites onto the prepared baking sheet, spacing them a couple of inches apart. With the back of a large spoon, create a well in the center of each egg white portion. Bake for 4 minutes. Remove the sheet from the oven and sprinkle a little fontina inside each egg white well and sprinkle some parmesan evenly over the outside edges of the egg white wells. Bake for 2–3 minutes, or until the egg whites are firmly cooked and starting to get golden around the edges, and the cheese has melted.

Remove the sheet from the oven. Crumble half of the prosciutto into the egg white wells, then carefully place one egg yolk in each well. Season the egg yolks with salt and pepper and bake for 3–4 minutes, until the yolks are cooked. Transfer the cloud eggs to serving plates and garnish with the remaining prosciutto crumbles and the basil.

EGGS IN PURGATORY

 SERVES 2–3

1 pound precooked Italian, andouille, or breakfast sausage links, thinly sliced

1 (26-ounce) jar Eat Happy Kitchen Tomato Basil Marinara or 2–3 cups Homemade Tomato Basil Marinara (page 30)

4–6 large eggs

Freshly grated parmesan cheese, for garnish (optional)

EGGS IN PURGATORY IS THE ITALIAN VERSION OF *shakshuka, a dish of slow-poached eggs in red sauce. I add sliced sausage for an extra hearty breakfast. You are free to add whatever veggies or spice mixes you want to the marinara. Throw in leftovers from last night's dinner, some extra marinara, and a few eggs, and you're ready to face the day.*

Heat a large, flat-bottomed sauté pan over medium-high heat. Add the sausage slices and sear for 2–3 minutes per side. Pour in the marinara and bring to a gentle boil.

Crack the eggs onto the surface of the marinara and turn the heat down to medium-low. Cover the pan and simmer for 8–10 minutes, or until the eggs are poached to your desired doneness. Serve immediately in shallow bowls, garnished with fresh parmesan, if desired.

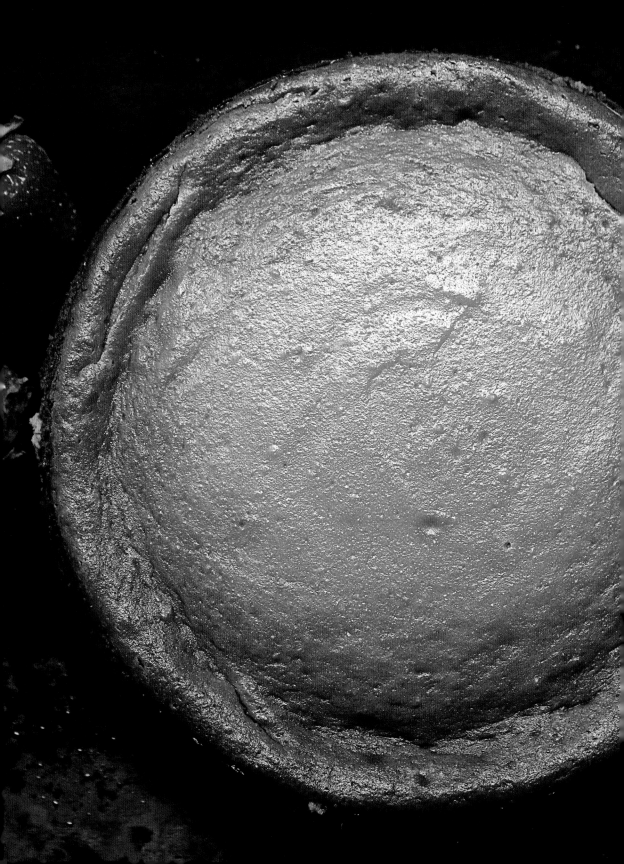

I DOLCI

I've talked about sweets so much in prior books, online, on podcasts, on my Substack recipe newsletter—heck, even at the beginning of this book! It bears repeating: The recipes in the following chapter contain sugar. They are desserts. I use real sugar, but you can trade that out for one you prefer, or even use artificial sweeteners or other sugar substitutes. I do not work with the sugar substitutes because I cannot tolerate them. But sugar is sugar, and the point of low carb is to get off sugar, right? Then life happens and you want to make a treat for the family or it's your birthday or whatever reason you want. In this chapter I have you covered with some classic Italian desserts made grain-free and with the least amount of sugar possible to make the recipe work.

For natural sugars, I prefer to use fruit, coconut sugar, honey, date syrup, or, frankly,

Ricotta Cheesecake, page 193

plain cane sugar or brown sugar (which is cane sugar coated in molasses). I repeat: Sugar is sugar, and your liver doesn't know the difference. I just want you to be able to enjoy a treat from time to time.

I choose to include a sweets chapter in all my books because the truth is that people who go low carb do end up eating some kind of sugar again at some point. I'd rather help you create a homemade treat than have you binge on store-bought crap. But if this chapter is triggering for you, rip it out and burn it immediately. There is so much love in every page of this book. I truly want you to succeed with all your goals and to live a happy life, whether you make a dessert or not.

RICOTTA CHEESECAKE

 SERVES 6–8

I LOVE CHEESECAKE. THIS IS THE THIRD·CHEESE-
*cake recipe I have published because, as far as I'm con-
cerned, there can never be enough cheesecake. This recipe
uses homemade ricotta as the star of the filling, which
gives the cheesecake a slightly different texture than that
of traditional New York–style cheesecake. I love to serve
it with berries, but I've also been known to sneak into the
kitchen and steal a slice to eat as is.*

To make the crust, preheat the oven to 350 degrees F.
Combine all the crust ingredients in a large bowl
and mix well until a dough forms. Press the dough into
the bottom and up the sides of a springform or pie
pan. Bake for 20 minutes, or until the crust is golden
brown. Let cool completely before adding the cheesecake filling. Leave the oven on or turn it back on to 350
degrees F when ready to bake.

Combine all the filling ingredients except the topping in a large bowl and mix until smooth. Pour the
filling into the cooled crust and bake for 1 hour 15 minutes, or until the center no longer jiggles. Remove the
cheesecake from the oven and let cool. Serve topped
with berries and whipped cream.

Pictured on page 190

CRUST

2 cups almond flour

8 tablespoons salted butter,
melted

1 tablespoon coconut nectar,
coconut sugar, or honey

1 teaspoon vanilla extract

CHEESECAKE FILLING

1 cup full-fat ricotta cheese,
homemade (page 35) or store-
bought

1½ pounds cream cheese, at room
temperature

¾ cup coconut sugar, coconut
nectar, or white sugar

½ cup crème fraîche or sour
cream

3 large eggs, beaten

1 tablespoon arrowroot powder

Juice of ½ lemon (about 1 tablespoon)

1 teaspoon vanilla extract

Sliced berries and whipped
cream, for topping

OLIVE OIL CAKE WITH LIMONCELLO GLAZE

 SERVES 8

YOU'VE SEEN ME REFERENCE MY FAVORITE OLIVE
*oil, Villa Cappelli, on my website and in the Introduction
to this book. I think it was the first 100 percent real olive
oil I had ever had. The late, great Paul Cappelli taught me
so much about olive oil purity, and he also taught me how
to make homemade limoncello. Limoncello is a famous
Italian lemon liqueur, and it's a national pastime in Italy to
argue about how one makes the best limoncello. Of course
I tweaked my recipe for limoncello to create a low-sugar
version, but that recipe is out of the scope of this book.
Instead, I'm borrowing from my limoncello recipe and making a glaze for this olive oil cake, in which I use none other
than the liquid gold that is Villa Cappelli olive oil.*

To make the cake, preheat the oven to 350 degrees F.
Lightly grease an 8 × 8-inch baking pan with olive
oil, then line the bottom of the pan with parchment
paper.

In a large bowl, whisk together the almond flour,
coconut flour, baking powder, and salt, making sure to
break apart any lumps.

Using a blender, food processor, or a small bowl and
a hand mixer, blend the olive oil and honey for 1–2 minutes until whipped and smooth. Add the eggs, one at
a time, and blend, then add the cream and vanilla and
blend until thoroughly combined. Pour the wet ingredients into the dry ingredients and whisk until smooth.
Pour the batter into the prepared baking pan. Bake for
25–30 minutes, or until a toothpick inserted into the
center comes out clean. When the cake is finished,

Recipe continues

CAKE

⅔ cup olive oil, plus more for
   greasing

2 cups almond flour

½ cup coconut flour

1 tablespoon baking powder

½ teaspoon salt

½ cup raw honey or coconut
   nectar, warmed until pourable,
   if necessary

5 large eggs

¾ cup heavy cream

2 tablespoons vanilla extract

GLAZE

Grated zest of 1 lemon (about
   1 tablespoon)

Juice of 2–3 lemons (4–6 tablespoons)

¼ cup honey, coconut nectar, or
   other sweetener of your choice

1 tablespoon vodka

1 vanilla bean pod *or* 1 teaspoon
   vanilla extract

allow it to stand for at least 10 minutes before you attempt to remove it from the pan. Run a knife along the sides of the cake to loosen it from the pan. Transfer the cake to a serving platter. Using a fork, pierce the top of the cake several times so when you pour the glaze over it, the cake will absorb more of the glaze.

While the cake is baking, prepare the glaze. In a small saucepan, heat the lemon zest, lemon juice, honey, and vodka over medium-high heat. Slit the vanilla bean pod lengthwise and scrape the beans into the saucepan, then add the pod too. Reduce the heat and simmer for 12–15 minutes, stirring occasionally, until a glaze forms. Remove the pan from the heat and discard the bean pods.

Use a spatula to evenly spread the glaze atop the cake, then allow the cake to sit for at least 1 hour for the glaze to become fully absorbed. Serve or cover and store in the fridge to serve later.

NO-CHURN OLIVE OIL GELATO

 YIELDS 3 CUPS

IF YOU HAVE A CHURN (AND PATIENCE) AND WANT TO *make a proper custard base for ice cream, by all means have at it. But for the rest of us, this no-churn gelato is a low-sugar summer treat that's quicker to make and fun to share. Plus, you can use the lightly sweetened condensed milk in any baking recipes that call for condensed milk, which is notoriously overly sweet when store-bought. Stracciatella means "little shred," and if you do that variation for this treat, the melted chocolate dropped into the almost frozen gelato will form little edible ribbons and bits that to me is better than chocolate chip any day of the week.*

Combine all the condensed milk ingredients in a small saucepan and bring to a boil over medium-high heat. Reduce the heat and simmer, stirring frequently, for 45–60 minutes, until thickened enough so the condensed milk sticks to a wooden spoon and drips off slowly. Transfer to a medium bowl and let cool to room temperature.

To make the gelato, in a large bowl using an electric mixer, beat the cream, vanilla, and coconut sugar until smooth peaks form. Do not overwhip the cream.

Add the olive oil and salt to the bowl with the condensed milk. Whisk in ½ cup of the whipped cream to soften the condensed milk mixture. Gently fold the condensed milk mixture into the remainder of the whipped cream until well mixed. Do not overmix as this will deflate the air in the whipped cream.

Pour the mixture into a freezer-safe container, cover, and freeze for 3–4 hours, or until it reaches the desired

Recipe continues

LIGHTLY SWEETENED CONDENSED MILK

2 cups heavy cream

3 tablespoons unsalted butter

1 tablespoon coconut sugar or other sweetener of your choice

1 teaspoon vanilla extract

GELATO

1½ cups heavy cream

1 teaspoon vanilla extract

2 tablespoons coconut sugar or other sweetener of your choice

3 tablespoons olive oil

¼ teaspoon salt

Stracciatella (recipe follows), chopped nuts, and/or sea salt flakes, for topping (optional)

firmness. Or, if making the stracciatella, remove from the freezer after 1–2 hours and follow the instructions below. If you're freezing the gelato overnight, remove it from the freezer to soften about 30 minutes before serving.

Serve topped with nuts or flaky salt, if desired.

STRACCIATELLA VARIATION

½ cup unsweetened condensed milk (see recipe above) or heavy cream

2 ounces 85% dark chocolate

Put the condensed milk in a small bowl.

In a double boiler or a small saucepan on low heat, carefully melt the dark chocolate, then whisk it into the condensed milk. Let cool but not harden.

After the gelato has been in the freezer for 1–2 hours, remove the gelato from the freezer and drizzle on the chocolate sauce. It will sink into the gelato in ribbons. Stir to break up the ribbons into little shreds. Return the gelato to the freezer until frozen to the desired consistency.

TIRAMISU

 SERVES 8

CLOUD BREAD LADYFINGERS

3 large eggs, at room temperature,
   separated

¼ teaspoon cream of tartar

2 tablespoons cream cheese, at
   room temperature

1 tablespoon coconut sugar,
   maple syrup, or honey

1 teaspoon vanilla extract

TIRAMISU

2 cups mascarpone cheese

½ cup brewed coffee

¼ cup coconut sugar

1 tablespoon rum

2 teaspoons vanilla extract

2 cups heavy cream

2 tablespoons unsweetened cocoa
   powder

1 ounce 85% dark chocolate

THIS IS A QUICKER VERSION OF THE ITALIAN CLASSIC
*dessert, omitting the egg yolks and using a version of
low-carb "cloud bread" for ladyfingers. Since cloud bread
is too delicate to submerge in coffee as you would with
traditional tiramisu, we add coffee to the cream. I use a
9 × 13-inch baking pan for a single-layer tiramisu, or you
can use an 8 × 8-inch pan for a multilayer tiramisu.*

To make the ladyfingers, preheat the oven to 325
degrees F. Line a rimmed baking sheet with parchment paper or nonstick aluminum foil.

In a medium bowl, combine the egg whites and
cream of tartar. Using a hand mixer, whip to stiff peaks,
then set aside.

In another medium bowl, combine the egg yolks,
cream cheese, coconut sugar, and vanilla. Using a hand
mixer, mix until creamy. Fold in the egg whites, being
careful not to overmix.

Spoon the dough into 3 × 1-inch strips on the prepared baking sheet. Bake for 10 minutes, or until the
ladyfingers are golden brown. Let cool for 2–3 minutes,
then gently loosen the ladyfingers from the parchment
paper to make sure they don't stick. Leave them on the
parchment paper to cool completely before assembling
the tiramisu.

To make the tiramisu, in a large bowl, combine the
mascarpone, coffee, coconut sugar, rum, and vanilla.
Using a hand mixer, mix until smooth.

In a cold stainless steel bowl, whip the cream until
soft peaks form, being careful not to overwhip. Fold the
cream into the mascarpone mixture until smooth.

Lay the ladyfingers in the bottom of a 9 × 13-inch baking pan. Add the cream mixture and smooth the top with a spatula. Refrigerate for 2–4 hours.

Sift the cocoa powder evenly over the top of the tiramisu, then grate the dark chocolate on top. Cut into squares and serve.

VANILLA PANNA COTTA

 SERVES 7–8

THIS AND THE RECIPE THAT FOLLOWS ARE TWO VER-
*sions of the beloved panna cotta, which means "cooked
cream" in Italian. Unlike a custard or pudding, panna cotta
uses gelatin as the firming agent, so pick up gelatin packets with no sugar added to have on hand to whip up this
smooth, creamy treat whenever you like.*

Lightly coat 7–8 custard cups or ramekins with olive
oil spray.

Pour the water into a small bowl and sprinkle the
gelatin over it. Do not stir. Let stand for 5 minutes.

In a medium saucepan, combine the cream, milk,
and sugar. If using a vanilla bean, split it lengthwise
and scrape the seeds into the pan, then add the pod
too. Cook over medium heat until hot but not boiling.
Add the gelatin mixture and whisk until dissolved. Give
the vanilla bean pod one final scrape to dislodge any
remaining beans, then discard it. If using vanilla extract, add it now. Pour the mixture through a fine-mesh
strainer into the prepared custard cups. Let them sit
for 10 minutes, then refrigerate for at least 4 hours and
up to 24 hours to set up before serving. If bubbles form
on the surface, remove them gently by skimming the
surface with a spoon. Serve with fresh berries.

Olive oil spray

⅔ cup water

2 packets unflavored gelatin
(about 2 tablespoons total)

2 cups heavy cream

2 cups whole milk

⅓ cup coconut sugar, coconut
nectar, honey, or other sweetener of your choice

1 vanilla bean *or* 2 teaspoons
vanilla extract

Fresh berries, for serving

CHOCOLATE PANNA COTTA

 SERVES 7–8

Olive oil spray

⅔ cup water

2 packets unflavored gelatin
(about 2 tablespoons total)

2 cups heavy cream

2 cups whole milk

⅓ cup coconut sugar, coconut
nectar, honey, or other sweetener of your choice

1 vanilla bean *or* 2 teaspoons
vanilla extract

3 ounces 85% dark chocolate,
chopped, plus extra for garnish

Raspberries, for serving
(optional)

THIS CHOCOLATE TWIST ON PANNA COTTA (PAGE 203) *is rich without being too sweet. The percentage listed on bars of chocolate refers to how much of the chocolate, by weight, is made from cacao beans. I use 85 percent cacao dark chocolate in my desserts because it is lower in sugar and deeper in flavor than bars made with less cacao.*

Lightly coat 7–8 custard cups or ramekins with olive oil spray.

Pour the water into a small bowl and sprinkle the gelatin over it. Do not stir. Let stand for 5 minutes.

In a medium saucepan, combine the cream, milk, and sugar. If using a vanilla bean, slit it lengthwise and scrape the seeds into the pan, then add the pod too. Cook over medium heat until hot but not boiling. Add the gelatin mixture and whisk until dissolved. Give the vanilla bean pod one final scrape to dislodge any remaining vanilla beans, then discard it. If using vanilla extract, add it now.

Turn off the heat and whisk in the chopped choc-olate until it's melted and smooth. Pour the mixture through a fine-mesh strainer into the prepared custard cups. Let them sit for 10 minutes, then refrigerate for at least 4 hours and up to 24 hours to set up before serving. If bubbles form on the surface, remove them gently by skimming the surface with a spoon. Shave ad-ditional chocolate over each serving, top with raspber-ries, and serve.

CHOCOLATE-DIPPED ALMOND BISCOOTS

 YIELDS 12–14 BISCOTTI

IN OUR HOUSE, WE CALL THESE "BIH-SCOOTS" *because of how our Italian grandparents pronounced and shortened the word biscotti. This bastardization of a common Italian food name should come as no surprise to anyone who refers to capicola as "gabagool." You know who you are! Biscotti are pretty tasty with coffee and easy to make grain-free with the use of almond flour. Decorate them how you like, but they always make a wonderful presentation.*

¼ cup plus 2 tablespoons slivered almonds

1½ cups almond flour

2 tablespoons coconut sugar or maple syrup

½ teaspoon salt, plus more for seasoning

1 large egg

1 teaspoon vanilla extract

Olive oil, for greasing

2 ounces 85% dark chocolate

Preheat the oven to 350 degrees F. Line a rimmed baking sheet with parchment paper, then spray it lightly with olive oil spray.

In a small nonstick sauté pan, toast the slivered almonds over medium heat, tossing often, until they're fragrant and starting to brown, 4–5 minutes. Transfer the almonds to a plate and let cool.

In a medium bowl, combine the almond flour, coconut sugar, salt, egg, and vanilla and mix until a dough forms. Fold in ¼ cup of the toasted almonds. Press the dough onto the prepared baking sheet to form a 3 × 12-inch rectangle that's ½-inch thick. Cut the dough rectangle into 1-inch strips. Separate the strips slightly so the biscotti will cook on all sides. Bake for 17–20 minutes, until golden brown. Remove the biscotti from the oven and let cool completely.

Finely chop the remaining 2 tablespoons toasted almonds and season them with salt. Melt the chocolate in a double boiler or a small saucepan over low heat and either drizzle it on the biscotti or dip the biscotti ends into the chocolate, then sprinkle the chopped almonds on the melted chocolate. Let cool completely and serve.

APPLE CROSTATA

 SERVES 3–4

CRUST

2 cups almond flour

1 teaspoon salt

1 teaspoon ground cinnamon

1 large egg

¼ cup salted butter, melted

1 teaspoon vanilla extra

FILLING

2 Gala apples, peeled, cored, and thinly sliced

2 Granny Smith apples, peeled, cored, and thinly sliced

3 tablespoons water

2 teaspoons lemon juice

2 tablespoons sugar, honey, coconut nectar, or other sweetener of your choice

1 teaspoon ground cinnamon

¼ teaspoon salt

⅛ teaspoon ground allspice

⅛ teaspoon ground cloves

⅛ teaspoon ground nutmeg

THIS TART WORKS GREAT WITH APPLES, PEARS, *peaches, plums, or whatever fruit you find that's in season. The crust is more of a crumble crust, and since we're not working with grains, which are more pliable, you will have to patiently press the crust up the sides of the pan. If it crumbles, you can press it back together easily. We are going for a rustic look, which helps when we are cooking grain-free!*

Preheat the oven to 350 degrees F.

In a medium bowl, combine all the crust ingredients and form into a dough. Press the dough into a 9-inch pie pan, pressing some of the dough up the sides of the pan. Bake the crust for 5 minutes. Let cool for 2–3 minutes, then press the edges even farther up the sides of the pan. Leave the oven on.

To make the filling, in a large saucepan, combine the apples, water, and lemon juice and cook over medium-high heat until the apples start to soften, 3–4 minutes. Stir in the sugar, cinnamon, salt, allspice, cloves, and nutmeg.

Pour the apple mixture onto the crostata crust. Fold the edges of the crust over the apple mixture. If the crust crumbles off, press it back into place. Bake for 15–20 minutes, or until the crust is starting to turn golden and the apples are soft. Let stand for 10–15 minutes before serving.

CHERRIES WITH VANILLA MASCARPONE

 SERVES 4

SEASONAL FRUIT WITH CREAM IS A FAVORITE DES-
*sert anywhere you go. This version uses fresh cherries,
which take a minute to cut and pit, and I highly recommend using prep gloves so your hands don't look like you
ran away guilty from a crime scene. This recipe also uses
blood oranges. Cherries are in season in June, yet blood
oranges are in season in January. If you are lucky enough
to find both fruits in your grocery store at the same time,
then congrats. If not, you can use a regular orange, and it
will be just as delish!*

1 pound cherries, halved and
　pitted

1 tablespoon sugar, honey,
　coconut nectar, or other sweet-
　ener of your choice (optional)

1 teaspoon grated blood orange or
　regular orange zest

2 tablespoons blood orange or
　regular orange juice

1 cup mascarpone cheese

¾ cup heavy cream

2 teaspoons vanilla extract

Fresh mint leaves, for garnish

In a large nonstick sauté pan, combine the cherries,
sugar (if using), orange zest, and orange juice. Simmer over medium heat until the cherries are soft, 4–5
minutes. Remove from the heat.

In a small bowl, combine the mascarpone, cream,
and vanilla. Whip the mixture with a whisk or hand
mixer until smooth. Serve with the cooked cherries,
garnished with mint.

ACKNOWLEDGMENTS

Thank you to the entire team at BenBella Books. What a unique adventure for me to have an anchor of such skilled and deft minds to guide and mentor instead of just me twisting in the wind. Claire Schulz, you are my fearless leader and gentle calm in the creative storm. And Ruth Strother and Karen Wise, you make me sound like the much more understandable version of myself that I wish I could be every day. To Sarah Avinger and Morgan Carr for the gorgeous cover, Endpaper Studio for the beautiful interior, and Monica Lowry and Isabelle Rubio for their shepherding of this book.

Thank you to Amy Collins, who nursed me through a bonkers book launch in 2019, got me out of cookbook retirement by 2022, and caused me to relight the spark of love for cookbook writing this present day.

Thank you to Scott Merritt and Roland Alonzi, the dream team that makes sure I present myself as much less idiotic than I feel at times. Your work, ideas, support, and perseverance are infectious.

Thank you to Greg Zellers, whose creativity keeps me and my brand integrity intact and on point. I literally couldn't have made it this far without you.

Thank you to John Schiaroli, whose mentorship, guidance, and belief in me when I had none in myself was the magic elixir to plowing ahead. LFG.

Thank you to Steven Crutchfield, proprietor of Villa Cappelli Olive Oil and dear friend. I know Paul is working through all of us to get the message of La Bella Vita out to the world. Thank you for helping me, inspiring me, and giving me that golden green elixir that keeps my motor running.

Thank you to Vinnie Tortorich, my podcast cohost, for never wavering on the low-carb message, for being a voice of reason in an obnoxiously loud space, and for keeping me motivated personally and professionally to never stop helping people who ask for it. I hope this book helps spread your   message even further.

Thank you to Todd Hauerland and Matt Kelley. There's no turning back now.

Thank you to all my friends, old and new, for their endless shoulders to cry on, words of encouragement, recipe brainstorms, and for just letting me be who I am.

Thank you to all the cookbook Happies and podcast community, without whom there would be no books, blogs, podcasts, or products. You all spreading the word is how this entire thing is built. I will always work to support you as long as I'm able.

Thank you to my kitchen right hand, Torri Anders, without whom this book would not exist. Your creativity, energy, and skills, mixed with your love and attention to details make you the only one I want to have in the kitchen with me.

Thank you to all the Vocinos, the Tarquinios, and all the family in between for nurturing me over the years through food. Thank you to my beloved Aunt Diane Evans and Uncle John Vocino, who archive and share the family recipes, secrets, and lore with me. Thank you to my father Tom and stepmother Caroline for all your support, with a special thanks to you, Dad. You are the best representation of the American Dream your father could've hoped for.

Thank you to Lucy, who is currently living all our best Italian lives in Rome. Thank you for being the epitome of what my grandparents intended for their Italian American progeny when they came to this country oh so many years ago. Your love of Italy and food helps inspire my food writing every day.

And finally, thank you to Loren, who stands by my side and eats all my food. Everyone with dreams this big should have a partner in crime like you.

INDEX

Page numbers in italics refer to photographs

216

ABOUT THE AUTHOR

Photo Credit: Joanna DeGeneres

Anna Vocino is a talented culinary personality and tastemaker who brings to the table a wealth of experience as a bestselling cookbook author, actor, stand-up comedian, podcast cohost, clean-eating expert, and founder of Eat Happy Kitchen, a natural food company making organically sourced, gluten-free, grain-free, and filler-free foods with no sugar added. Anna has created hundreds of recipes that have appeared in her bestselling cookbooks, *Eat Happy* and *Eat Happy Too*, and on her website, AnnaVocino.com, Substack, and her popular Instagram account. As a respected voice within the clean-eating community, Anna can deftly transform almost any recipe into a healthy version of the dish without sacrificing taste. Anna's recipes and expertise on everything from spices to kitchen appliances have been featured in *Women's Health, Parade, Consumer Reports, Real Simple, SELF Magazine, Allrecipes*, and other consumer media outlets.